Super Pre
Classic Ley

John Banks

Includes Photographs by G H F Atkins and from the Senior Transport Archive

© 2001 J M Banks

ISBN 1 898432 34 1

Front Cover: Titan, Tiger and fashionably dressed lady in a typically idealised artist's townscape as used in Leyland advertising in the early 1930s. *(STA)*

Inside Front Cover: Classic Leylands have survived into the 21st Century in some numbers. Here we see a former Brookes Brothers Lioness LTB1 and a Thames Valley TD1 Titan at a 1960s Brighton vintage vehicle rally. *(Both: John Senior)*

Rear Cover: A fine portrait of one of the many Titans which gave sterling service north of the border. **WG 5480** now wears the striking Western SMT black and white livery. *(John Banks)*

Inside Rear Cover: Leyland for all time? History was not quite to bear out that promise made in 1931 on a Leyland clock near Blackpool, though there were to be another 50-odd years. *(STA/BCVM)*

Title page: Yorkshire Traction No. **282 (HE 4724)**, photographed in March 1930, is typical of the Titans a couple of years or so after the launch of the model, by which time the Leyland-built 48-seat lowbridge bodywork was equipped with an enclosed rear platform and staircase. This gleaming, brand new machine displays the rather small destination indicator screen and the rearward-hinged driver's cab door. The vehicle was withdrawn and sold for scrap in 1938, but many others survived for 20 years and more. *(STA/BCVM)*

Opposite page: By 1938, the New South Wales Department of Road Transport had increased its Titan fleet to 95. The bodywork was beginning to look less British and was taking on the "Sydney look" which became so familiar through the rest of the 1930s, the 1940s and into the 1950s on Leyland and other makes of chassis. This 1937 TD4 had a Waddington body. *(STA)*

Below: An impressive line-up of nine Tigers and a Cub in the fleet of L J Keys Ltd, Auckland, New Zealand in 1936. *(STA)*

CONTENTS LIST >>

Introduction	7
Municipal Leylands	16
Company Leylands	37
Independent Leylands	55
Leylands for Leisure	72
Leyland demonstrators	86
Leyland trolleybuses	93
Leylands in London	103
Leylands overseas	114

THE 'TITANIC' SIX-WHEELER

*The "Titanic"—a type offered for seating capacities
greater than those afforded by the "Titan"*

INTRODUCTION

Whatever might be said of the merits (and demerits) of such as Crossley, Daimler, Dennis, Guy, Karrier, Maudslay, Thornycroft and many another (for, in 1926, there were around 60 passenger chassis *marques* among which the British bus or coach operator might choose), there can be little doubt that there were but two major manufacturers of bus and coach chassis - Leyland and AEC - in the United Kingdom during the decade or so that preceded the outbreak of war in September 1939. Furthermore, the classic late-1920s and 1930s products of both Leyland Motors Limited and The Associated Equipment Company Limited originated from the fertile brain of one of the Century's foremost engineers: the great George John Rackham.

The two companies had rather different beginnings. Whereas the roots of AEC lay in the vehicle-building arm of the London General Omnibus Company Limited from 1908 to 1933 (though not incorporated as "The **A**ssociated **E**quipment **C**ompany Limited" until 13th June 1912), and could be said to have had in the quarter-century to 1933 a somewhat cushioned existence as a result of its captive market as a member of the Underground Group (there was, indeed, a period when it would have gone under but for the guaranteed orders from its parent), Leyland was an independent business from its earliest years in the last decade of the 19th Century as The Lancashire Steam Motor Company to well beyond the Second World War. When Leyland had *its* bad patch in the early 1920s, there was no such cushioning from a supportive guardian: but Leyland survived its losses all the same and went on to great things. That both giants came together as constituents of the gargantuan British Leyland in the 1960s and that both eventually disappeared is well-known, although those comparatively recent events do not concern this book, which commemorates those classic chassis and body combinations built to serve the world's passenger transport undertakings, great and small, before the Second World War.

Leyland appointed John Rackham Chief Engineer in the summer of 1926, but he was unsettled and wished to move to the warmer south. *"I do not altogether like the idea of living in the dreary North of England permanently,"* he wrote, adding, *"The North of England is bearable in summer but in winter London is the only place to live in,"* in his letter to George Rushton of AEC on 14th March 1928 enquiring about a possible vacancy. The lines of Rackham's letter were almost certainly meant to be read between. Before joining the Southall manufacturer as Chief Engineer on the 1st August 1928, he gave Leyland's possibly ungrateful management - in the Tiger TS1, Titan TD1 and their derivatives - a range of new models which would propel the Lancashire vehicle builder successfully into the new decade and set a pattern for its vertical-engined products: products that would hold sway into the 1950s until paralleled and eventually consigned to oblivion by underfloor- and rear-engined chassis.

The nineteen-twenties was a decade in which the British public service vehicle underwent a profound change. It opened barely a quarter-century after the infamous "man with the red flag" had been rendered legally unnecessary. Nonetheless the average bus or lorry chassis in 1920 bore more than a passing resemblance to one from 1905. They would have been even more alike had the "war to end all wars" not broken out following the assassination of a certain Grand Duke in Sarajevo in 1914. That conflict was to become the first mechanised war. Not only did it create an insatiable demand for self-propelled transport, its urgent needs contributed in no minor way to motor vehicle research and development; ironically, improvements thus accruing were in some cases, as is dispiritingly often the case with developments provoked by emergency situations, not to find general use until after the war had ended.

Another, perhaps more tangible, result of the mechanisation of the military was that the latter did not want such huge fleets of vehicles once it had stopped waging war. Thus vast numbers of ex-military vehicles poured onto the postwar market. In some cases these were much as they had ended their war service; others were purchased by professionals within the motor industry, to be thoroughly refurbished prior to sale into a postwar civilian career. Leyland was in the forefront of this type of activity although the exercise took it to near-bankruptcy.

The vehicles themselves, however good or bad as they faced the brave new world fit for heroes, were still pretty much "first generation" machines: solid-tyred, open-cabbed, chain-driven, with engines giving a poor power-to-weight ratio. If they were passenger vehicles, they might well have had no fixed roof if single-deck, and definitely not if double-deck.

"If they were passenger vehicles, they might well have had no fixed roof if single-deck, and definitely not if double-deck." The Blackpool-registered "Seagull" char-à-bancs **FR 1716** *admittedly had a canvas hood, which could be raised in the event of inclement weather, but the Cornwall-registered double-decker* **AF 2370**, *with the fleetname "Pioneer", was uncompromisingly open-topped. Most such vehicles had tarpaulin covers with which upper-deck passengers could cover their lower limbs but, in truth, by the time of these turn-of-the-decade scenes, things had not advanced a great deal in passenger comfort since before the First World War. (STA/BCVM)*

Whether in terms of carrying capacity for goods vehicles or of passenger seating in buses, their legal loadings were modest. The construction of motor vehicles of all types and their use on public roads in those days attracted, as it always has and no doubt always will, an ever more burdensome load in the shape of restrictive legislation. This was particularly onerous in the Capital, where responsibility for approving and licensing motor buses lay with the Commissioner of Police of the Metropolis. This duty was delegated to the Public Carriage Office at Penton Street in North London. Whilst it is not always true to say that what London did today the rest of the world did tomorrow, it was not unknown for licensing authorities in the provinces to take their cue from the PCO.

To say that the latter was unimaginative and resistant to change would be understating the case. Among the more printable words used to describe it may be found "reactionary", "hidebound" and "conservative". Apart from keeping a tight control over vehicle dimensions, effectively delaying the introduction of proper width of seat, leg room and gangway, the Public Carriage Office at one time or another set its face resolutely against such civilising influences as rear-view mirrors, enclosed driving cabs with windscreens, roofs on upper decks, enclosed platforms and staircases, doors on front-entrance single-deckers and pneumatic tyres for some time after such things had been perfected and proven safe and of benefit to the travelling public and bus crews alike. Despite the baleful influence of the PCO beyond the boundaries of its bailiwick, buses and coaches outside London sometimes benefited from such design advances a little earlier than did those in the Capital.

That, by 1927, John Rackham's new Leyland Titan double-decker could emerge as a cohesive design incorporating an enclosed cab and windscreen, a roof and pneumatic tyres, speaks volumes for the progress, practical and political, being made during the decade. The Titan still had an outside staircase, but not many months were to pass before that anachronism, too, became a thing literally as well as figuratively of the past. Rackham's move to AEC in 1928 meant that a parallel series of models would soon emerge as strong competition for the Leylands, particularly after AEC was separated from London General's successor, the LPTB, from 1st July 1933. Even then AEC had the enormous advantage of an agreement with London Transport to supply the majority of its motor buses. Leyland fought the good fight, however, and succeeded in winning LPTB orders for about 300 motorbuses in what remained of the 1930s. Added to the 295 Leylands acquired from various sources by the LPTB, those orders ensured a surprisingly healthy Lancastrian presence in such a staunch AEC stronghold. There was no such LPTB/AEC agreement over trolleybuses and Leyland supplied over 800 in the same period.

So it was that, despite the efforts of Crossley, Daimler, Dennis and their colleagues, many company and municipal fleets up and down the country were restocked with ultra-modern Rackham-designed or inspired buses and coaches. The independent sector, too, fell prey to the siren-song of the salesmen from Southall and up near Preston; whereas the battle for orders from the large fleets was fairly evenly balanced (although without AEC's virtual monopoly on supplying London Transport, it probably wouldn't have been), perhaps Leyland had the best of it with the independents, many of whom remained loyal until Leyland chassis were no longer available.

The Leyland Titan is often referred to as "Rackham's masterpiece"; if the truth be told, however, almost any one of his designs could be thus described; furthermore, Leyland had a pre-Rackham masterpiece in the Lion, which had appeared in 1925. This was a simple, sturdy chassis on pneumatic tyres with a willing four-cylinder petrol engine which was lively and economical; with around 30 seats, and offering comfort and reliability, it was just what operators wanted and it sold, almost without the intervention of salesmen, in large numbers.

When Rackham was appointed, he was given a brief to design a new range of chassis without reference to what had gone before. The Lion and its bonneted equivalent, the Lioness, were successful (and would, in fact, continue in production and be steadily improved through Rackham's tenure and beyond for several years) but the same family's double-decker, the Leviathan, was ungainly, top heavy, usually solid-tyred and in need of replacement. That replacement was the Titan.

Long-distance coaching was coming into its own in the last part of the twenties and would expand rapidly in the early thirties. Some ambitious services were offered and many not only survived but prospered. The Lion was perhaps a little basic for such work, but in 1927 Rackham's new Tiger answered the need. An imposing machine with a six-cylinder engine (petrol, of course, at that time), capable of

Above: In a postwar design, The Mid-Cheshire Motor Bus Company Limited's No. **8 (MA 4098)**, a 36hp 30-seater of 1920, had left behind the ex-military image and progressed some of the way to providing weather protection for both passengers and driver, though his access at both sides was still open; in this picture a passenger appears to be risking the breeze. This vehicle passed to North Western on 1st January 1925 and was withdrawn in 1928. (STA/BCVM)

Below: An otherwise very similar body on a 1922 vehicle for the The Kendal Motor Bus Company Limited went that last step and completely enclosed the driving compartment by means of forward-hinged doors. The Kendal concern was taken over by Ribble in April 1930. (STA/BCVM)

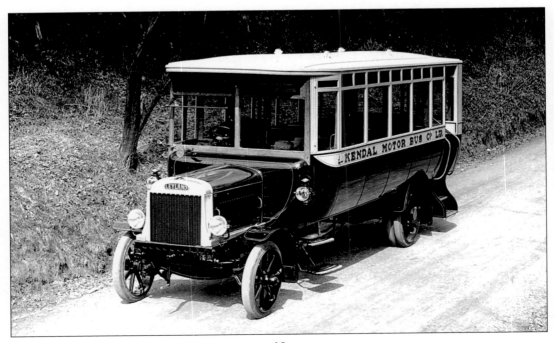

*By May 1923, fleet number **19** (**CK 3357**), a 39-seat SG7, of Pilot Motors was clearly a stepping stone to the Lion of 1925, although there were still solid tyres. CK3357 had a full-width cab, popular then but soon to lose ground to the half-cab, which permitted quicker and easier engine changes. This vehicle passed to Ribble in October 1926 and was withdrawn in 1930. (STA/BCVM)*

maintaining respectable cruising speeds over long distances, it wafted passengers along the Great North Road and other arteries in near-silent comfort, not to say luxury. The bread-and-butter work for most operators was less glamorous, however.

It involved relatively short routes in and between towns and cities: routes that often ran to an intensive timetable that might see the bus filled to capacity two, three or more times during a single journey. Or tram, indeed: many tramway systems were then either at their zenith or not far past it. Trams, however, were falling into disfavour. Never mind that many a city in continental Europe continued, and still continues in the new Millennium, to shift its population around by ever more efficient tramway networks, in Great Britain they had to go and are only now making an expensive comeback. The reason was fairly simple: investment in new buses to replace trams would be on a far smaller scale than that needed not only to improve and restock tramway systems and fleets but merely to make good the ravages of under-investment in earlier decades.

Such short-haul city and inter-urban work found its ideal tool in John Rackham's Titan, also first seen in 1927. *"Bury a tram with a Titan"* was the battle-cry of Leyland's sales department, and large fleets of them were built up by operators from Scotland to the south coast. The Titan was found to have another advantage: its low height, achieved through the ingeniously designed "lowbridge" layout, usually seating around 48, and its sprightly performance from a 6.8-litre petrol engine and four-wheel brakes, meant that it could do work in more rural areas, work which usually included diversions along country byways to serve villages and hamlets, hitherto best served by smaller chassis, often of foreign manufacture, fitted with single-deck bodies of much more modest seating capacity.

The Lion, Tiger and Titan families spawned a variety of offspring and had a number of zoological relations: the Lion begat the Lioness, the Tiger the Tigress and the Titan the Titanic; there were Leverets, Cheetahs and Badgers; the Cub appeared, and then the Lion Cub. By the time in the later 1930s of the three-axle, twin-steering Gnu and Panda, the underfloor-engined FEC Tiger and the rear-engined REC Cub (the latter pair developed in close cooperation with London Transport), the Rackham influence was wearing a little thin; such advanced designs, each in its own way of considerable merit, did not have the success that the Rackham designs had found.

Each type and sub-type appearing over the decade was identified by a model-code: the Titan, for example was originally the TD1 but had progressed to the TD7 before war stopped production (a TD8 was planned but never built); the Tiger ran from TS1 to TS11 in the same period. Some designations were rare or never appeared: the TD6 Titan, for example, was sold only to Birmingham Corporation; and there were no TS9 or TS10 Tigers.

There were trolleybuses, too, the earliest based on the Lion and the Titan; the latter had genuine if non-functioning radiators, as well as bonnet-sides and half-cabs, which were visually indistinguishable from those of their internal-combustion-engined brethren.

As if the astonishing numbers and variety of Leylands to be seen about the highways and byways of the United Kingdom were not enough, the Company had a thriving export market where most of its models, as well as various export-only derivatives, could be seen. It will be the task of this book to survey that World of Leyland, through vehicles built from John Rackham's time up to the Second World War. The photographs are taken mainly from the fabled Geoffrey Atkins and Senior Transport Archive collections, with help along the way from a number of smaller though no less valuable collections, each acknowledged separately in the captions.

A *caveat*: such things as engine cubic capacity and transmission details may be mentioned in passing in the pages of this work, but its *raison d'être* is not to be a technical treatise: it is rather that of attempting to evoke the scene in cities and towns, main streets and country lanes when what transport students of a certain age are pleased to call "traditional" buses and coaches thronged the bus stations and thoroughfares.

And here it is time for a confession: in his formative years, that is to say those wherein a boy sits up and takes notice of his local bus and coach fleets and gradually becomes through his adolescent and teenage years ever more enthusiastic, the writer was never "a Leyland man". The comment made at the start of these introductory notes about AEC and Leyland being the two front-runners in bus production - perhaps in the world; certainly in Great Britain - before the Second World War, holds true for a number of years after it, too. And this was reflected in youthful partisanship. Just as, on the end of a railway platform on a summer Saturday morning, young train-watchers preferred ex-

Two stages in the pre-Rackham development of the Leyland double-decker. Above is an Over-Type demonstrator of circa 1922. Although it is known to have run in Keighley, little is known about it. The Leviathan, the last pre-Titan Leyland double-decker, was basically a solid-tyred vehicle typical of conventional thinking at that time. Some were fitted with pneumatic tyres, although not Crosville's LG1 No. 220 (FM 3791) (below). New in 1926, it was withdrawn in 1931. (Both:STA/BCVM)

*Here is the quintessence of the transitional period, when there were Leviathans and even older machines still in front-line service, but gradually being pushed to the less glamorous end of the fleet by the incoming Titans. In the picture above, taken in the garage of Preston Corporation on 14th March 1933, PLSP2 Leviathan No. 65 (**CK 3907**) dominates the photograph; it had been new in December 1927, was fitted with pneumatic tyres in May 1931 and withdrawn in 1934. Another Leviathan, PLSP1 No. 64 (**CK 3745**) of 1926, hides at the back, but the purpose of the picture was clearly to show the new Titans. In this case they are TD2s, and fleet numbers 45, 48 and 50 (**CK 4641**, **CK 4644** and **CK 4647**) are visible. All had 53-seat highbridge bodies by English Electric and survived to 1947 (No. 50) and 1950. The Peterborough Traction Company Limited was one of the constituents of the new Eastern Counties Omnibus Company Limited, formed in July 1931. Its 1925 open-topped, 48-seat Leyland LB5, No. **AB4** (**FL 4216**), seen below at Skegness in July 1929, was typical of many, modernised to a greater or lesser degree, which survived, though not for long, into the Titan period. FL4216 passed to Eastern Counties in 1931 and was immediately withdrawn. (STA/BCVM; GHFA)*

LNER locomotives to those of the former LMS or vice versa, so off the rails and on the tarmac was there a marked split between the "AEC" and "Leyland" camps.

This obviously had much to do with what the local operators ran. The writer's exploratory years were spent in a city almost equally divided: the municipal fleet was firmly AEC and the Company was Leyland. That he and one or two friends in those days preferred the AEC whilst others favoured Leyland is not easy of explanation. Perhaps it was the preselector gearbox (though the earlier AECs had clutches and gear levers); perhaps it was an indefinable feeling that the AECs were more sprightly performers than the Leylands; perhaps it was simply in the shape of the radiator; more likely it was a combination of all those aspects. There was a seven-day wonder when a visiting cousin from Coventry forthrightly poured scorn on us all. He understandably worshipped at the shrine of Daimler and considered his local *marque* superior to either of ours.

Maturer years brought a wider appreciation and understanding of the honourable place fought for and maintained by all the manufacturers - major and minor - in a competitive industry. Leyland was an institution: it was as English as cricket or afternoon tea and made a comparable impression throughout the world.

The preparation of the captions in the pages that follow owes much to the writer's friend of many years, Ron Maybray. Ron is a skilled researcher into vehicle history and is ever generous in making his comprehensive fleet records available to the writer. Quite simply, it is the truth that this book could not have been written without his enthusiastic help. Alan Townsin has cast his expert eye over the proofs, much to the benefit of the text. John Senior is owed grateful thanks for always being instantly ready to be of help and guidance with his vast knowledge of the British bus industry, for giving the writer the freedom of his unique photographic and documentary archive *(STA)* and for checking the proofs. Philip Battersby has given his usual expert help. Geoffrey Atkins *(GHFA)* has generously allowed many of his superb photographs to be used - something which automatically enhances any book. Grateful thanks, too, to the British Commercial Vehicle Museum *(BCVM)* for courteously allowing reproduction of material in the Senior Transport Archive which originated with the old Leyland Motors Limited.

Other sources of photographs are individually acknowledged and I am most appreciative of Brian Thackray's permission to quote from the 1928 Rackham letter now in his collection. David and Mary Shaw have read the proofs and have, as always, spotted more than one cunningly concealed typographical error. Books, magazines and miscellaneous publications, too numerous to mention individually, collected and read over the last forty years, have also contributed much, directly or indirectly. The publications of the PSV Circle and The Omnibus Society never cease to offer invaluable information for any work such as this, and the debt owed them is once more acknowledged. For readers anxious to learn more about the Leyland story, the books listed below are indispensable. Many of them are long out of print and seldom seen on the shelves of dealers in second-hand books; when they are however, they should be snapped up without hesitation.

Jack, D: *The Leyland Bus.* Transport Publishing Company, 1977. *(440 pages; a comprehensive history, produced with the full cooperation of Leyland.)*

Jack, D: *The Leyland Bus Mark II.* Transport Publishing Company, 1984. *(524 pages; a revised and updated edition.)*

Townsin, Alan: *The Best of British Buses No. 1 - Leyland Titans 1927-1942.* Transport Publishing Company, 1981. *(96 pages.)*

Townsin, Alan: *The Best of British Buses No. 3 - Leyland Tigers 1927-1981.* Transport Publishing Company, 1981. *(96 pages.)*

Booth, Gavin: *Leyland Buses in Camera.* Ian Allan Ltd, 1981. *(128 pages.)*

Martin, Gavin: *London Buses 1929-1939.* Ian Allan Ltd, 1990. *(144 pages, includes technical and operating details of prewar London Transport standard Leyland classes.)*

Glazier, Ken: *London Buses Before the War.* Capital Transport, 1995. *(160 pages, a general survey that includes the prewar Leylands, with some mention of the ex-independent LPTB stock.)*

Bruce, J Graeme and Curtis, Colin H: *The London Motor Bus - Its Origins and Development.* London Transport, 1977. *(144 pages, includes a description of London's Leylands.)*

John Banks
Romiley, Cheshire
July 2001

MUNICIPAL

Leylands

Almost, it seemed, in the thirties, every town and city had its Leylands. Some fleets had nothing but, others a smattering among other makes. In this section, municipal pride from the four corners of the United Kingdom is on display, starting with Lincoln's LT1 Lion No. **5 (VL 1263)**, fitted with a locally built Applewhite body, seen in historic surroundings on 22nd June 1931. VL 1263 survives in preservation. *(STA/BCVM)*

The Pre-Rackham Standard

Above: Leyland sometimes chose names that could be thought unsuitable. "Leviathan", in most of its dictionary definitions, has the connotation "huge" or "monstrous", or both: and thus Leyland's double-decker of that name often seemed, with its great height and ungainly appearance. Edwin Chadwick (1800-1890) looks down from his plinth onto Bolton Corporation's 52-seater No. **11** (**BN 9354**) in 1926. The glistening wet, cobbled surface and the narrow section solid tyres were a lethal mixture but at least the upper-deck passengers had a roof.

Below: Whereas the Leviathan was rapidly outshone by the Titan (Bolton's No. 11 had gone by 1931), the more aptly named Lion soldiered on for a decade or more, albeit with major redesign. The original PLSC came in two versions, the PLSC1 and the longer PLSC3. Wallasey's No. **1** (**HF 4109**) was a PLSC1, with 32-seat Leyland bodywork. It ran until 1935 and then went on to work for a fairground showman. *(Both: STA/BCVM)*

Lionesses in Town

The normal-control layout for large goods and passenger vehicles was still popular at the start of our period and would not be entirely eclipsed until the postwar Bedford OB and its Austin and Commer lookalikes went out of production. The look of a high-grade private car may have had a stronger appeal when forward control was still unfamiliar in many parts of Britain. York Corporation's No. **13** (**DN 9039**) *(left)* was a 1927 PLC1 with Leyland 26-seat bodywork, clearly considered an economical proposition even when compared with the forward-control PLSC1 which could seat six more passengers. DN 9039 was taken over by the new York-West Yorkshire undertaking in September 1935. Blackpool also favoured the PLC Lioness: No. **21** (**FR 7354**) of 1926 *(below)* heads a line-up of six. *(Both: STA/BCVM)*

Trams and Low Bridges Conquered

Above: It is hard today to realise just what an advance the lowbridge bus was. The railway companies had spread their bridges over most highways and many of the byways of the country in the 19th Century and users of road motor traffic in the 20th had to live with the consequences. Even horse-drawn loads were occasionally baulked by a low bridge and gangs of locals with shovels augmented their income by lowering the crude road surfaces of the day. Until John Rackham's TD1, bus operators could not squeeze two decks under many such bridges. Even with the TD1 there were problems: this photograph perhaps set out to suggest that passengers had been prone to hysteria as this particular bridge approached them, but in fact the painted message had been provided for the benefit of upper-deck passengers on open-top trams. St Helens Corporation No. **70 (DJ 4835)** shows how it was done. The Leyland-bodied TD1, a 1931 delivery, was withdrawn in 1940. *(STA/BCVM)*

Below: A bit of tram-burying in Preston in November 1932. One of Preston's TD2 Titans, No. **44 (CK 4640)**, passes a gang of navvies, some of whom have relaxed to pose for the camera, busily engaged in removing tram trackwork. Preston's highbridge TD2, English Electric-bodied, was rebodied by the same firm in 1940 and survived into 1950. *(STA/BCVM)*

Coachwork Variety in Wallasey

Above: Wallasey Corporation's TD1 No. **20** (**HF 5349**), with a New Brighton-bound tram in the background and a PLSC Lion in front. This was the operator's first Titan, delivered in April 1928, which epitomised the all-Leyland chassis/body combination. *(STA/BCVM)*

Left: Wallasey's 1931 TD1 No. **67** (**HF 7443**), on the other hand, had two-door bodywork by Eastwood & Kenning, outside whose Trafford Park, Manchester, premises this view was taken when the bus was brand new. The front exit was intended to speed unloading at the Seacombe Ferry terminal. Number 67 lasted eight years and was withdrawn in 1939. *(STA)*

Titans and Stone Sets

Above: Although both tramlines and granite sets survive into the new Millennium, they are, in combination, perhaps more readily associated with the earlier years of the 20th Century. The abiding image of shiny new Titans in town centres is of them running over the tracks and stones. Preston's 1928 TD1 No. **66 (CK 4050)** eases downhill towards the camera in 1928 with a grandiose example of Victorian municipal pride as backcloth.

Below: In another 1928 view, Birkenhead Corporation's TD1 No. **90 (CM 8075)** is very much the new-fangled device rubbing shoulders with the old in the shape of a Leviathan and a selection of trams. The Leviathan, which has both covered top and pneumatic tyres at the front only, is No. **50 (CM 6606)**, a 1926 machine which lasted just five years in Birkenhead's service. The 1928 Titan managed ten. Its open staircase was enclosed in 1933. *(Both: STA/BCVM)*

21

Titans in Glasgow

Above: This picture had to be included for the remarkable cameos of pedestrians dashing across the road in front of Glasgow Corporation's 1928 TD1 No. **93** (**GE 2428**). The two girls have seen the camera but the formally attired gentleman with both feet off the ground has not. Other pedestrians are waiting patiently by the kerb which suggests that the Titan was moving, perhaps under the control of a point-duty policeman.

Below: Number **127** (**GE 2462**) from the same Glasgow Corporation batch is less hampered by jaywalkers as it heads for Knightswood. Both scenes, with trams and other buses prominent, as well as horse transport, are redolent of the late 1920s. *(Both: STA/BCVM)*

Glasgow Variety

Above: The Leyland Titanic totalled 46 examples in all its versions (TT1 to TT5) in the decade it was in production. The three-axled AEC Renown fared much better with nearly 1,600, although without London Transport's fleet of 1,439 examples things might have been more evenly balanced. This impressive 1931 example, bearing Glasgow's livery, was merely tried there as a demonstrator and then sold to Sheffield.

Below: By 1937 the Titan model had moved on to the TD5 and Glasgow had some with Weymann, of Addlestone, bodies in what had become the standard, 56-seat, rear-entrance layout for many operators. Number **504** (**BGA 70**) was new in November 1937 and was withdrawn in 1951. *(Both: STA/BCVM)*

Titanics in Bury

Above: What a superb social document this is. In a Bury scene from 23rd July 1936, Titanic TT3 No. **55** (**EN 6054**), one of five similar buses, blends, despite its bulk, surprisingly well into the fabric of the town centre. The couple in the foreground engaged in earnest conversation could be a local doctor and his wife; the mums and grannies have their infant charges in up-to-the-minute perambulators; passengers and bus crews wait in and around the bus shelter: they all combine to evoke a more relaxed age. *(STA/BCVM)*

Below: On the same day, No. **52** (**EN 6051**) gave an uninterrupted view of its unusual centre-entrance body. Built by English Electric, it provided seats for 60 passengers. *(STA/BCVM)*

Stockport Corporation

Above: In a wonderfully evocative scene taken at Gatley, near Cheadle, in Cheshire, on 4th June 1936, Stockport Corporation's TD4c Titan is discharging suburban mothers and children. The small "c" in the designation indicated a vehicle fitted with torque-converter transmission, and the legend "Gearless Bus" on the radiator and the torque-converter header tank alongside the Autovac above the nearside-front mudguard confirm that No. **157** (**JA 6213**) was so fitted. This bus, new in 1935, lasted a respectable 23 years and was withdrawn in 1958.

Below: Another Stockport TD4c, from the following year, was No. **177** (**JA 7577**), seen at Manchester in May 1936. Its Leyland 52-seat bodywork shows considerable styling advances over the previous year's vee-front version from the same factory on JA 6213. JA 7577 was withdrawn in 1960. *(STA/BCVM; GHFA)*

Municipal Portraits

Above left: Enthusiasm for the Titan spread to all corners of the country as municipalites everywhere took it up. Plymouth added this example, No. **131** (**DR 9071**), a TD1 with standard Leyland 48-seat lowbridge bodywork, to its fleet in August 1931. The bus was damaged by enemy action in 1942 and was rebodied by East Lancashire Coachbuilders. It lasted thus until April 1951.

Above right: Plymouth, as a naval stronghold, was in the forefront of the onslaught from German bombers in the Second World War, which caused many lives to be lost, many buildings to be damaged or destroyed, and wrought havoc with the Corporation's bus fleet. There was not enough left, after it was struck by bombs in April 1941, of 1935's Weymann-bodied lowbridge Gearless Titan TD4c No. **87** (**JY 5005**) for it to be thought worth rebuilding or rebodying.

Left: Yet another TD4c. This example, bodied as a highbridge 52-seater by English Electric, was No. **35** in the Blackburn Corporation fleet. **BV 4117** entered service in 1935, had an uneventful life running around Blackburn for 14 years until 1949, when it was withdrawn and sold for further use as a mobile shop in the Manchester suburb of Northenden. *(All: STA/BCVM)*

In these views of 1938 TD5 Titans, Wigan Corporation's No. **96** (**JP 2965**) can be seen to have had Northern Counties bodywork to the piano-front outline as used by Leyland up to 1933, while Oldham's No. **174** (**ABU 859**) had a Leyland body boasting rather more modern lines. These buses lasted in service respectively until 1953 and 1956. *(STA/BCVM)*

Mist and Sunshine

Above: A misty 1931 day in St Helens fortunately did not put off the photographer when the Corporation's No. **70 (DJ 4835)**, a TD1 which we have already seen demonstrating its low-bridge negotiating abilities *(see page 19)*, whispered up to a busy bus stop. The condition of the bus and the presence in the crowd of gentlemen in bowler hats and bus inspectors suggest that this might have been the vehicle's first day in service.

Below: The sun was out, in sharp contrast to the St Helens scene, in Cardiff on 18th March 1932. Cardiff Corporation's No. **66 (UH 7175)**, a 1929 Titan TD1, was outside the premises of Griffiths & Millington Limited, who were contractors for advertising on, among other things, buses and trams. *(Both: STA/BCVM)*

Oldham Corporation

The concept of municipal pride was touched on in the introduction to this section *(see page 16)*. It would be hard to find a better illustration of such pride than these Oldham views. The depot scene *(above)*, apart from including 1937 Titan TD5 No. **147 (ABU 365)**, reveals a spotless working environment which - then - was by no means uncommon. Oldham's No. **122 (BU 9523)** *(below)* was a 1936 TD4, seen in immaculate condition in a street scene notable for its cleanliness and lack of litter. Both buses were 56-seaters with English Electric highbridge bodywork. They were withdrawn respectively in 1950 and 1949. *(STA/BCVM)*

Classics in Quantity

Above: Leicester City Transport's Nos **303-309** (**BRY 265-71**) were Gearless TD5c Titans delivered in November 1937. All these Leyland-bodied highbridge 56-seaters were withdrawn in 1950. Three of them, Nos 306-8, had an interesting afterlife with the South Western Omnibus Company, of Colombo, Ceylon (and its successors), for whom they ran for at least another eight years. *(STA/BCVM)*

Below: Buses with centre entrances were not necessarily unusual in the nineteen-thirties but Blackpool Corporation is the operator that springs to mind when such a layout is considered. It was a fleet with flair, and much of that flair was directed towards catering for day trippers and holidaymakers to the resort. This wonderful line-up of Burlingham-bodied 53-seat TD3 Titans was photographed when new in August 1933; they were the first TD3s to reach an operator's fleet. The buses pictured, from left to right, are Nos **86**, **85**, **89**, **88** and **87** (**FV 3561/0/4/3/2**). All were withdrawn in 1949 and scrapped in 1951. *(STA/BCVM)*

Bottom: In September 1937 Geoffrey Atkins produced a picture that compares well with that on page 21. The trams have gone, their tracks are there but filled in with tarmac, and the buses comprise four Massey-bodied highbridge 54-seaters, including Nos. **231/2** (**BG 5513/4**) on 1937 TD5c chassis and No. **217** (**BG 4390**), a 1936 TD4c, as well as a 1931 TD1, No. **152** (**BG 200**). *(GHFA)*

Titans in the Townscape

Above: Now and again a photograph produces an image so evocative that the onlooker is almost physically transported back in time. This is one of them: the bus is the Todmorden Joint Omnibus Committee's 1928 TD1 Titan No. **7 (WW 6798)**, growling up a narrow street on its way to Burnley through a townscape redolent of the era and of the industrial north. *(STA/BCVM)*

Below: The little Austin 7 saloon, the car that sounded the death-knell for the cyclecar and even the motorcycle combination, is the real star of this August 1931 picture, but we can spare more than a passing glance for Leicester's Brush-bodied Titan TD1. Number **57 (JF 1533)**, a 1931 highbridge 50-seater, was lent to London Transport in 1941, ran for Barton Transport after the war and ended up with a building contractor. *(STA/BCVM)*

Lincoln Corporation

Above: Lincoln was an early user of the Titan. This one is a 1928 TD1, No. **29** (**VL 845**), seen - doubtless in first gear - on a rather punishing combination of sharp bend and steep gradient. The standard Leyland 48-seat open-staircase body was later enclosed and the vehicle was withdrawn in 1949. The photograph was taken in June 1931. *(STA/BCVM)*

Below: Almost as long-lived in the Lincoln fleet was TD5 No. **56** (**AFE 374**), with the metal-framed Leyland body then current, which lasted two decades from 1938 to 1958. It was about six weeks old in this June 1938 picture of it emerging from Lincoln's famous Stonebow arch. *(GHFA)*

Municipal Rareties

Above: The elusive TD6 version of the Titan was only supplied to Birmingham Corporation. A batch of 50 was supplied in 1939, although there is some doubt about their exact designation: strictly, they were type TD6c, having gearless transmission. The 52-seat rear-entrance bodies were by Leyland and the first of the batch, No. **1270** (**FOF 270**), was scrapped in 1952. *(GHFA)*

Below: Along with "Leviathan", though for different reasons, the name "Titanic" was possibly ill-chosen. The tragedy of the sunken liner was scarcely 15 years in the past when it was selected for Leyland's flagship double-decker, which in the event was almost as unfortunate as its nautical namesake. Doncaster's No. **73** (**DT 7813**) was a 1936 TT3c version, with Roe 60-seat bodywork: an undoubtedly impressive machine. It was brand new when photographed in September 1936. *(GHFA)*

Municipal Tigers

Above: **ERA 96** was No. **24** in the Chesterfield Corporation fleet from December 1937 to 1955. It was a 32-seat Tiger TS8 with Leyland-built bodywork. In this July 1940 view it was at Beetwell Street, Chesterfield, complete with wartime additions to its livery. *(GHFA)*

Below: Neighbouring Derby Corporation's fleet number **47** (**RC 2347**) was a 1935 Gearless Tiger TS6c, new in January of that year. It had a Brush 35-seat body and was withdrawn in 1941. It had been the only Leyland in a predominantly Daimler fleet. This September 1936 picture was taken in Victoria Street, Derby. The lady pedestrian with shopping basket swinging was having to skip nimbly out of the path of the two youthful cyclists. *(GHFA)*

Corporation Cubs

Above: The Kingston-built Leyland Cub was a successful contender for what was perhaps the equivalent of today's "midibus" market. It found favour with a wide variety of operators, including some municipalities, in both coach and bus form. Lytham St Annes **TJ 136** was fleet number **2**, a Burlingham-bodied KP2 20-seater new in January 1933, which was withdrawn in 1943. *(STA/BCVM)*

Below: Douglas Corporation No. **8** (**CMN 709**) was a rather later Cub based on the KPZ1 model, new in March 1938 and fitted with Park Royal 20-seat bodywork. It was withdrawn in 1954 but survived in various guises for a further decade before being sent for scrap. *(STA/BCVM)*

Titans Diverted

As the threat of war loomed and eventually became a reality, the bus-building industry was faced with a comprehensive rescheduling of its production potential, mostly directed towards military requirements. One of the first problems was that production of buses, even those partly built, was halted by decree from on high. When some sort of order was restored, it was realised that such vehicles ought to be completed and released to hard-pressed operators whose capacity was often being stretched far beyond prewar levels by the needs of the war factories and armed services personnel. The buses did not necessarily go to the operator which had placed the order for them. A case in point was the bodies for four Western SMT Leyland-bodied TD7 Titans, which were diverted to Hull Corporation in May and June 1942. Registered GKH 381-4, they were given fleet numbers 200-3. We illustrate Nos **200/2** in postwar years. The Western SMT destination screen arrangements, so unlike Hull's own, remained throughout their Hull service. They were withdrawn in 1960. *(R K Evans; R F Mack)*

COMPANY

Leylands

<< Previous page: Company operators were as keen as their municipal colleagues in restocking their fleets with new Leylands. Company vehicles strayed further from their bases than did buses on municipal routes; thus they were seen and - all too infrequently - photographed in rural as well as urban surroundings. The Tiger was a TS2 in the West Yorkshire Road Car Company fleet. Number **505** (**PY9489**) was fitted with Leyland's own 31-seat bus bodywork. New in January 1929, it had been taken over with the business of Frank Reynard, who traded as the "Lion Bus Service", of Easingwold, in March of that year. This photograph was taken on 1st July 1931, and No. 505 was rebodied as a 31-seat coach by Eastern Counties in 1936. In that form, and renumbered 556, it ran until withdrawal in October 1949. In the background of this fine York Minster scene is York Corporation's 1930 Crossley Eagle No. **25** (**VY2228**), which would in 1934 join the Tiger in the West Yorkshire fleet when the York-West Yorkshire Joint Committee came into being. *(STA/BCVM)*

This page: New to the LMS Railway in January 1929, this PLSC3 Lion *(above)* with LMS Derby-built 32-seat body was transferred to the Sheffield Joint Committee C fleet in 1930. Number **14F** (**CH 7905**) was withdrawn in 1935 and sold to Lincoln Corporation as fleet number 11. It became an ARP ambulance in 1940. The photograph was taken at Pond Street, Sheffield, in June 1934. Hants & Dorset specified open-tops for some Short Bros-bodied 1928 TD1s, represented by No. **230** (**TR 5053**) and two others in an April 1929 line-up *(below)*. Number 230 was sold to the Southern Railway in 1938. *(GHFA; STA/BCVM)*

Standard and Non-Standard Titans

Above: The coachbuilder Christopher Dodson, of Willesden, in north-west London, was best known as a staunch supporter of, and supplier of coachwork to, the independent operators who ran in competition with the London General Omnibus Company Limited in the Capital. When in 1933 the LGOC was - in effect - converted into the LPTB and the independents were compulsorily taken over by that body, Dodson's market collapsed and he closed his business down. He had been responsible for equipping many Titans for various of the independents during the first five years or so of the model's existence, but it was less common to find Dodson-bodied Titans outside London. Dodson's London bodies were built to suit the Metropolitan Police; in comparison with the Leyland standard, they were archaic and ungainly in appearance. **VS 1084** of the Glasgow & Port-Greenock Tramways Company was a 1928 highbridge 54-seater.

Right: The Leyland version is shown on a 1930 East Kent 51-seater, registered **JG 978**, which was photographed in Canterbury in August 1931. It lasted in service until 1947 and was scrapped by East Kent in April 1949. *(Both: STA/BCVM)*

<< Opposite page: Tram-burying and low bridge-mastering was a part of the Company operators' philosophy no less than it was of that of the Municipalities. The BET tramway system in Gravesend was comprehensively buried by TD1s in the late 1920s. Numbers **305/11 (KP 3398/404)** of Gravesend & District *(upper)* glide around the streets with little more fuss than a hissing from the petrol engines' carburetters and a whine from the gearbox to replace the clanking of the recently departed trams. In the lower picture, 1928 TD1 No. **130 (TE 2773)** of Lancashire United Transport (an independent, to be accurate, but as the biggest such, very much "company" in appearance and outlook), gives another convincing demonstration of the Titan's ability to thwart the railway companies' low bridge legacy. *(Both: STA/BCVM)*

This page: In a Leeds view taken in June 1932, passengers pose for the camera before boarding the previous year's Leyland-bodied TD1 No. **175 (HD 4360)** of the Yorkshire Woollen District Transport Company Limited. In contrast with the longevity in their original owners' fleets of some early Titans, this one was withdrawn after only eight years by Yorkshire Woollen. It served two subsequent owners - Caledonian and Western SMT - for rather longer, from 1940 to 1950, however, before being scrapped in December 1952. *(STA/BCVM)*

Yorkshire Woollen District

Yorkshire Woollen District was a staunch supporter of the Leyland *marque*, buying little else between the Dennises of the mid 1920s and the utility Guy Arabs of the war years. These July 1935 views were taken to illustrate Dewsbury's annual holidays, when local factories closed down and crowds fled to resorts such as Blackpool or Bridlington to refresh themselves for the next twelve months' grind. The vehicles featured, all dating from 1932, were not exactly holiday transport, and were no longer at the newer end of the fleet. Number **191 (HD 4602)** was a Lion LT5, bodied by Leyland as a 32-seat service bus, and the double-deckers were TD2s with Leyland, on No. **205 (HD 4616)**, or Roe, on No. **244 (HD 4806)**, bodies. *(STA/BCVM)*

Railway-operated motor coaches

United Automobile Services Limited, of Lowestoft, from the factory that in 1936 would become Eastern Coach Works Limited, supplied twin-door 26-seat coach bodies with canvas roofs for these Tiger TS2 private hire vehicles operated by the London, Midland & Scottish Railway. The vehicles were new in July 1929 and later passed to the Hebble Motor Services fleet. **UR 3763** *(above)* was photographed on the Promenade in Scarborough in the summer of 1929. The parking of coaches on the promenade was stopped by Scarborough council in the early postwar period. In the picture below **UR 3764**, in a different livery and with the hood closed, was at an unknown location on 11th July 1929. *(GHFA; STA/BCVM)*

East Yorkshire Motor Services Limited

Above: On 28th June 1938 East Yorkshire's Brush-bodied Tiger TS6 No. **254** (**RH 8923**) was turning into Paragon Square, Hull, having just left Paragon coach station. It was on its way to Goole via the quaintly termed "Caves" and Howden. "Caves" referred to the separate villages of North Cave and South Cave. The Tiger was being followed by two of Hull Corporation's Weymann-bodied Daimlers. *(STA/BCVM)*

Below: At the other side of the square, on the same day, Brush-bodied Titan TD4 No. **278** (**ARH 766**) was about to enter the coach station at the end of its inward journey. The arched roof matched the gothic profile of Beverley Bar, through which many East Yorkshire routes ran. The photographer caught a passenger standing on one leg having just jumped off the moving bus. *(STA/BCVM)*

Lincolnshire Road Car Company Limited

Above: Lincolnshire was a great user of the Leyland Cub, well suited to the company's many rural services. In this 1937 photograph, No. **LC503** (**FW 8856**), an oil-engined KPZO1 new in May of that year, picks up some rather self-conscious passengers in what looks very much like a posed view. The Brush-bodied 20-seater lasted in Lincolnshire service until 1951. Another Cub, **FW 7094**, was going the other way. *(STA/BCVM)*

Below: Lincolnshire took three TD1 Titans in 1931 for use on the 32-mile Spalding to Skegness via Boston combined service. Number **LT189** (**FW 2230**) was the last of the trio. New in May 1931, it lasted until 1954, albeit rebodied by Willowbrook and fitted with a Gardner 5LW oil engine in 1943. *(STA/BCVM)*

Eastern National

Above: Roof-mounted route-number boxes were not common outside London. Eastern National specified the arrangement on some 1937 lowbridge TD4 Titans bodied by Eastern Coach Works. Number **3656 (ENO 934)** served Eastern National until May 1952 when it was transferred to the United Counties Omnibus Company.

Below: An earlier product from the Lowestoft coach factory, then under the control of Eastern Counties, for the Eastern National fleet was No. **3424 (AEV 794)**, a 1933 Tiger TS4 with unusually high-built 26-seat coach bodywork. The front-entrance body was rebuilt with a rear entrance and 31 service-bus seats during the war and the vehicle was withdrawn from service in 1951. *(Both: STA)*

More Lowestoft-built coachwork

Above: Leyland chassis with Lowestoft-built bodies were common before the war. Among the most attractive was this TS7 Tiger with Eastern Counties rear-entrance coachwork, United Counties No. **404** (**VV 3774**), seen here in Nottingham when brand new in 1935. *(GHFA)*

Below: Eastern Counties built bodywork for its own fleet, of course, as well as the wide variety manufactured for other operators. Fleet number **AT135** (**NG 3879**) was a 29-seater, new in April 1933, which would have been whisper-quiet as it pulled away when new but was converted to diesel power using a Gardner five-cylinder unit in May 1937. An extensive rebuild by Eastern Coach Works in 1943 helped the vehicle to survive to 1950. *(GHFA)*

Devon General

Above: Devon General's No. **161** (**DV 4891**) was a 31-seat Tiger TS2 with front-entrance Hall Lewis bodywork. It was new in 1930, the year of this photograph, and passed to Western National (Royal Blue) in 1936. *(STA/BCVM)*

Below: Number **114** (**BDV 5**) in the Devon General fleet had a complicated history. A Harrington-bodied Tiger TS7, it was new in 1936 as a 32-seat service bus. It was rebuilt by Tiverton Coachbuilders in 1944 and later passed to Ribble Motor Services who had it rebodied by Burlingham. This seaside view of it was taken in the summer of 1936; the body style was characteristic of this operator in the later 1930s. *(GHFA)*

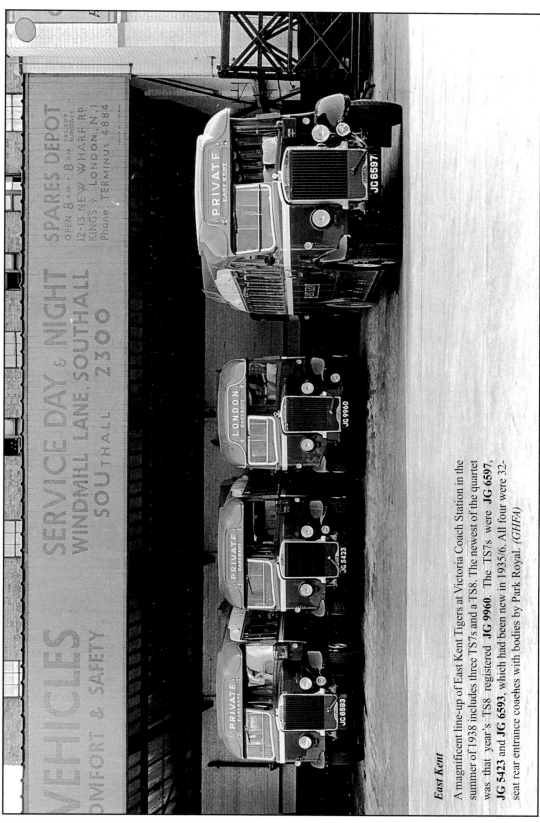

East Kent

A magnificent line-up of East Kent Tigers at Victoria Coach Station in the summer of 1938 includes three TS7s and a TS8. The newest of the quartet was that year's TS8 registered **JG 9960**. The TS7s were **JG 6597**, **JG 5423** and **JG 6593**, which had been new in 1935/6. All four were 32-seat rear entrance coaches with bodies by Park Royal. *(GHFA)*

London Victoria

Above: A pair of Southdown TS7 Tigers inside Victoria Coach Station in May 1939. Nearest the camera is No. **1156** (**CUF 156**), a 1936 Burlingham-bodied 32-seater, which was waiting to leave for Gosport and Fareham. The cream roof was an unusual feature. Alongside, and shortly to leave for Brighton, was the previous year's No. **1113** (**CCD 713**), also a 32-seater, this time with Harrington coachwork more typical of this fleet. Both survived into 1956 and both went on to work in contractors' fleets. *(GHFA)*

Below: Maidstone & District No. **687** (**KJ 5432**) was another Harrington-bodied machine. A Tiger TS4, it had 31 seats and a centre entrance. New in 1932, it had gone by 1940. A July 1937 photograph. *(GHFA)*

East Midland portraits

Above: The fleet of East Midland Motor Services Limited retained for many years, via its livery, a link with United Automobile Services Limited, of which it had originally been a subsidiary. Whereas United suppressed the yellow and brown livery in 1930 in favour of red and cream, East Midland kept it until well into the postwar period. Leyland-bodied TS7 Tigers of 1935/6, **B11/24** (**BAL 611/ BRR 924**), demonstrate what was effectively still the 1928-30 United livery - one of the smartest colour schemes in the country.

Right: East Midland, like its neighbour the Lincolnshire Road Car Company, had few double-deckers in the prewar period, and most of what there were came from Leyland. Number **D6** (**BAL 706**), a Leyland-bodied lowbridge 53-seat TD4 Titan of 1935, was one of six which had been preceded only by two 1932 AEC Regents. The hard-edged outline of the Clayton destination box sits rather awkwardly on the vee-front body. *(All: STA/BCVM)*

Cubs in the Valleys

Above: From this angle the resemblance of the normal-control Cub to a large luxury car of the period is obvious. Western Welsh's No. **216** (**KG 7064**) was a 1936 KP3. *(STA/BCVM)*

Below: Leyland KP1 Cub **PL 2223** may well have been the first passenger example of the Cub, with chassis number 4, dating from 1930 and appropriately registered in Surrey, the home county for the Kingston factory which was responsible for building the Cub. It is seen at that works, ready for dispatch to the West Monmouthshire Omnibus Board as fleet number **6** in February 1931; it was to remain there until 1939. It then served Monmouthshire County Council as a mobile casualty unit. The Leyland front-entrance body had 20 seats. *(STA/BCVM)*

Western SMT

Above: Among the most striking of coaches plying the main roads to London were the black and white creations of Western SMT. Fleet numbers were not used by this operator until 1949. The TS7 shown, registered **CS 2007**, was a 1935 32-seater with Leyland coachwork, a vehicle that was later rebuilt as a double-decker. It was at Grantham in August 1935. *(GHFA)*

Below: Western SMT's **CS 5225** was also a TS7 Tiger, new in 1937. It had fully fronted Burlingham coachwork seating 32. It features in a busy scene inside Victoria Coach Station alongside a pair of East Kent Tigers. The picture was taken in the summer of 1937. *(GHFA)*

Scottish six-wheelers

Above: The Leyland Gnu totalled eight chassis in 1937-9. Perhaps with a name like that it didn't deserve to proliferate. This example, No. **P411** (**WG 6608**) in the Alexander fleet, was a 1937 Earls Court Show exhibit. The Alexander 40-seat bodywork had the entrance ahead of the front wheels. It ran for Alexander until 1945 and then for Stanhope Motor Services until 1954. *(STA/BCVM)*

Below: Alexander's **P436** (**WG 6676**) was also a 40-seat Gnu, but the operator-built body was finished in Alexander's Bluebird coach livery. This one passed to Truman, of Shirebrook, in 1945 and was then with Stanhope Motor Service from 1952 to 1954. *(STA/BCVM)*

The independent sector in the decade and a half before the war was a mixture of contrasts: intense pride, often outdoing the most fiercely proud municipality, frequently involved calling upon the services of the local photographer, polishing up every vehicle in the fleet until they gleamed, driving them all to a suitably photogenic pastoral location, and recording them on film. On the other hand, it was possible to see - particularly before the 1930 Road Traffic Act began to bite - the most amazing antedeluvian rattletraps, which ought never to have been on the road. The best of the independents, however, fielded fleets that put many of the bigger people in the shade, or - at the very least - equalled them, for comfort and quality of service. Thus the independents, too, bought Leylands, often at the rate of only one or two or so a year, and some fine, modern fleets were built up. Many of them, alas, were swallowed by the company operators who, sometimes literally if contemporary press reports of court cases are to be believed, ran them off the road. Gower Vanguard Motors (1920) Limited TD1 No. **23 (WN3744)**, photographed on 13th April 1931, was carrying the registration number (UP5438) of a Leyland LT2, new in May 1931 as fleet number 16 to Wilkinson, of Sedgefield - a long way from the Gower Peninsula. Clearly there had been a mix-up in the Leyland factory. WN3744 passed to United Welsh as No. 566 in January 1939 and lasted well into the postwar years.
(STA/BCVM)

INDEconnectENT
Leylands

The Leyland Badger

Above: Fleet number **5** (**CK 4144**) in the fleet of Viking Motors, of Preston, was a 24-seater based on the Badger TA3 goods chassis, which had an engine and other features in common with the Lion LT1. The straight frame of this model ensured a rather high profile in what was a slightly uncomfortable mating of goods chassis and passenger coachwork. The photograph was taken on 20th June 1929. *(STA/BCVM)*

Below: Another Badger, this time a 1930 TA4, in the fleet of S & J Wood, of Blackpool, who traded as "Seagull". This one was a coach with three slam doors on the nearside. The Seagull fleet achieved some celebrity in the early postwar period when Burlingham's "Seagull" coach body was named for it. *(STA/BCVM)*

Independent Lionesses

Above: Seen on a private hire assignment to Alton Towers in July 1931, **RA 3075** was a 1927 PLC1 Lioness in the fleet of F H Doughty, of Brimington, Derbyshire. This view emphasises the proportion of the overall length taken up by the set-back radiator and bonnet; the consequent loss of passenger space was obviated on more compact forward-control designs, but the bonneted passenger vehicle took a long time to die. *(GHFA)*

Below: **CW 6956** was a similar, 1926, vehicle in the fleet of Wright Bros (Burnley) Limited, which ran under the fleetname "Pullman Service". Although this and the Doughty vehicle were used on private hire and excursion duties, they were built to little more than service bus specification. *(STA/BCVM)*

Luxurious Lions

Above: The PLSC Lion of 1926-9, even with standard bus body, was similarly often found on prestige work to seaside and other attractions, though scarcely equipped to the standard which the nineteen-thirties would introduce as *de rigueur* for such vehicles. The fleet of D W Burn, trading as Grey de Luxe, of Kingston-upon-Hull, was a household name for quality and reliability in that city until it disappeared into the grasp of a competitor some decades after this picture was taken. Grey de Luxe Lion **KH 4071** was on Marine Drive, Scarborough, in July 1934. *(GHFA)*

Below: **CW 8266**, also a PLSC, was another "Pullman Service" vehicle of Wright Bros (Burnley) Limited. New in 1928, it had unusual Strachan & Brown 32-seat coachwork with opening roof and luggage rack. The firm was acquired by Ribble in 1934 and absorbed into its Standerwick coaching subsidiary in 1935 *(see also page 80)*. *(STA/BCVM)*

Nottinghamshire independents

Above: Another household name, further south, in Nottingham, was that of G W Dennis, trading as "Robin Hood". Their first vehicle to the contemporary modern coach specification was a TS4 Tiger, **VO 7400**, new in March 1932 with 31-seat coachwork by Strachans (Acton) Ltd. In this May 1935 view it was at Huntingdon Street, Nottingham. *(GHFA)*

Below: Wass Bros, of Mansfield, was an enthusiastic Leyland user and in August 1938 took into its fleet these two 32-seat Willowbrook-bodied Lion LT7 coaches registered **BNN 716/ 7**. They were running on hire to the Trent Motor Traction Company Limited when photographed at Huntingdon Street, Nottingham. This is an August 1938 picture taken when the coaches were but days old.*(Both: GHFA)*

Nottinghamshire independents

Above: Leah Bros, of Huthwaite, bought **AAL 486** in July 1933. The vehicle was of great interest as being the prototype Tiger TS6 - the first of a new generation of Leyland passenger models. The Leyland-built coach body was also a prototype. It ran as a Leyland demonstrator in Ribble livery on trade plates and was photographed thus in January 1933. This view at Bathley Street, Nottingham, was taken circa 1936. *(GHFA)*

Below: Skill's, of Nottingham, Leyland KP3 Cub **TV 4847** was new in July 1931 with 20-seat rear-entrance bodywork by A Dixon Limited, of West Bromwich. Still with Dixon's publicity in the window, the vehicle was at Nottingham Corporation's Parliament Street depot in 1931. *(GHFA)*

West Riding

Above: The West Riding Automobile Company Limited, of Wakefield, was another independent of such size and style that it was often thought to have been under the aegis of one of the big groupings. Number **420** (**HL 7110**) was a 1935 Gearless Tiger TS7c with Leyland metal-framed 32-seat bodywork. It lasted with West Riding until 1949. In this June 1936 view it was at Barnsley. *(GHFA)*

Below: Torque-converter transmission was standard in this fleet and was also specified in 1938 for No. **525** (**HL 8623**), a TS8c with Roe bodywork seating 32. The provision of a roof-mounted luggage carrier, hardly a stylish addition in this case, was unusual by 1938. The deep proportions are understood to have been to accommodate musical instruments; "band coaches" were fairly common at the time. The vehicle was at Whitby railway station in June 1938. *(GHFA)*

Independent Titans

Above: The South Wales independents were a hive of interesting activity for some decades. One of the smartest such fleets was that of Rees & Williams Limited, of Tycroes, whose No. **12 (TH 2091)** was a 1931 Titan TD1 in the classic combination with Leyland's own enclosed-platform body. The vehicle was brand new in this picture taken on 4th November 1931. *(STA/BCVM)*

Below: The "big group company" impression again, in a Leeds view of West Riding's No. **20 (HL 5325)**, a 1932 TD2 Titan with Roe bodywork. This 48-seater had a centre entrance and was one of 45 purchased to replace the West Riding tram fleet and painted red rather than the usual green. New in May 1932, it was withdrawn in 1948 from the West Riding fleet but survived for at least another decade. *(STA/BCVM)*

Independent luxury

Above: For a May 1932 registration, this Tiger TS4 with Beadle 32-seat coachwork had a rather antiquated look. Number **16** in the fleet of Heath, Doncaster, trading as "B & E", **DT 3697** was nonetheless a very luxurious machine which plied the highways between London and Bradford. It was on such a journey when photographed at Huntingdon Street, Nottingham circa 1936. *(GHFA)*

Below: Another fine modern coach which had a slightly vintage air about it was Santus-bodied Tiger TS6 **CK 4760**, dating from June 1933. This 32-seater was new to Hodgson, of Preston, and ran under the fleetname "Bon Chaunce". It was photographed at Skegness. *(GHFA)*

Express Cub

A. Chinery, of Acton, Sudbury, in the county of Suffolk, who traded as "Corona Coaches", bought this neat and tidy KP3 Cub in November 1931 for use on his London to Stowmarket express service. Number **16** (**GV 883**) was a 24-seater with Duple coachwork. These pictures of it in rather begrimed condition after a winter's work were taken on 31st May 1932. *(Both: STA/BCVM)*

All-weather Tigers

In 1928/9 the Lowestoft factory of United Automobile Services Limited produced some convertible bodies of distinctive design fitted to Tiger TS2 chassis. Two went to the LMSR *(see page 43)* and four similar vehicles were completed for stock for the Nottingham sales depot of Leyland Motors. Two were quickly sold to local operators. **VO 1417** *(above)* went into the fleet of the Ebor Bus Company, of Mansfield, in May 1929 and similar vehicle **VO 1010** *(below)* was bought by Swain, of Stanton Hill, who traded under the fleetname "Supreme". They were both found in a Skegness coach park on the same day in July 1929. The detail differences in the shape and decoration of the radiators is noteworthy. *(Both: GHFA)*

Sunshine and water

Above: This immaculate 32-seat LZ5 Cheetah with Plaxton body, **BWF 147**, was new in 1939 to Mr J France, who traded as Ideal Motor Services, of Market Weighton, in the East Riding of Yorkshire. It is seen when still very new on private hire work at a race meeting. *(STA/BCVM)*

Below: Barton Transport, of Chilwell, was a fleet in which Leylands figured prominently, both bought new and acquired second-hand. Number **160 (VO 8411)** was a 1933 Lion LT5 with Leyland 35-seat front-entrance bus bodywork, which ran for Barton until 1948. In this watery scene taken in January 1936 it was heading for Kegworth on service 10. *(STA/F W Stevenson)*

The Leyland Tigress

Above: Qualifying for this section only in that its owner, Southdown Motor Services Ltd, exercised considerable "independence" of spirit when specifying it, this vehicle was a rare Burlingham-bodied Tigress of 1936. This model was basically a female version of the Tiger TS7. Tigresses were perhaps more popular in Leyland's export markets than they were at home. Number **1823** (**CUF 323**), seen here at Central Workshops, Portslade, in March 1949 being prepared for the forthcoming summer season, lasted until it was withdrawn and sold for scrap in 1952. *(Denis Clark Collection/Eric Surfleet)*

Photo Call

Below: A fine example of "polish 'em up and take their picture": these are eight Tigers in the fleet of Arthur Christy, of Bolton, photographed in hazy Lancashire sunlight on 10th May 1932. *(STA/BCVM)*

Lions on Parade

Above: Looking brand new, but in fact about a year old, Allen's of Mountsorrel Lion LT1 No. **14** (**UT 5503**), which had been new in 1929, was photographed at Drummond Road, Skegness, in July 1930. The Leyland bus body had 35 seats. *(GHFA)*

Below: One of the glories of the Senior Transport Archive, especially in pictures originally supplied as publicity material by the old Leyland Motors Limited, is the proportion of photographs taken of buses and other traffic in normal service. The star of this view is undoubtedly the AA patrolman on his motorcycle combination as he leads a pair of Lancashire United LT1 Lions through Spring Gardens, Buxton. Number **173** (**TE 7074**) - as was the one following - was another 1929 LT1. The 30-seat front-entrance body was by Davidson. TE 7074 lasted until 1960 after conversion to a trolleybus pole-erector lorry. *(STA/BCVM)*

Cub coaches

The concept of a vehicle used solely as a luxury coach reached its zenith in the 1930s. Already by May 1932 this KP3 Cub *(above)* of Progress Pullman (Jackson's Progress Motors, of Chorley), registered in Lancashire's "TF" series, with the fleet number **4**, was well on the way. There is a single, car-type slam door and the seating is padded and sumptuous with headrests. There was probably not a luggage boot at the back, and curtains were not specified. The body was built by Santus Motor Body Works, Wigan. A year or more later, however, **AGY 908** *(below)*, a forward-control SKP2 of July 1933 from the fleet of Metcalfe's Pullman Motorways, of Regent Street, London, had comparatively modest seating, room for luggage on the roof, and the same slam-type door, but at the front. The body, manufacturer unknown, carried the legend "Dolomite Motorway": was the vehicle - despite its basic seating - perhaps used for Continental touring? *(Both: STA/BCVM)*

Armchairs on wheels

Above: Harrington-bodied **XJ 9438**, a 32-seat 1933 Tiger TS6 in the fleet of Connolly's Tours, of Gorton, Manchester. It was at Trent Bridge, Nottingham, circa 1934. *(GHFA)*

Below: **AOF 191** in the Allenways, Birmingham, fleet was almost contemporary with Connolly's XJ9438. Another TS6, with a rear-entrance Burlingham 32-seat body, it was new in the late summer of 1934. In these two vehicles can be seen a further step: curtains are now fitted, though the luggage is still carried on the roof, with all the attendant dangers and inconvenience of such a system. *(STA/BCVM)*

Scottish fleets

Above: The classic original Titan TD1, with 48-seat lowbridge open-platform body from Leyland's own body factory. This one was **SN 4655**, fleet number **16** in the fleet of A & R Graham Ltd, of Kirkintilloch. The vehicle was rebodied by Cowieson as a highbridge 52-seater circa 1937 and passed to Walter Alexander & Sons when that concern bought the Graham business in July 1938. *(STA/BCVM)*

Below: A unique vehicle: **WG 9519** was the only Leyland Panda built; it differed from the Gnu in having an underfloor engine. It was a centre-entrance 45-seater in the Alexander fleet (No. P683) with whom it entered service, after being bodied by the operator, in September 1941, although the chassis was built in 1939. In June 1946 it passed to Truman, of Shirebrook, with whom it is seen in this picture, as fleet number **24**. It passed to East Midland in 1956 but was not operated and was sold to Aston, of Marton, in 1957. It was scrapped in 1963. *(GHFA)*

Leylands

FOR LEISURE

Tram, Tower, Trippers and a Tiger: it couldn't be anywhere else... Blackpool Promenade on 12th September 1931 was host to a TS3 of S & J Wood Ltd, who traded under the fleetname "Seagull". **FV1827** was typical of the leisure coaching market at the start of the nineteen-thirties. Seats, although of leather and extremely comfortable, were not yet high-backed, and there were no curtains; as the decade progressed those extra touches of luxury would become commonplace. Leisure in those days for the majority of the population meant one annual holiday, probably of a single week, although enterprising proprietors had for some years been building up excursion and private-hire work. Seagull's Tiger had a full-length canvas roof and no fewer than three slam doors: a specification not so very far removed from that of the *chars-à-bancs* of the 1920s. In this section we shall see a wide variety of Leylands catering to most aspects of leisure travel in an age which did not have the somewhat mixed blessing of television and whose citizens who were also car-owners were distinctly the minority. *(STA/BCVM)*

Lionesses for hire

Above: The original PLC Lioness sold well enough to justify further development, and the result was the LTB1, a fine example of which was **UA 8918**, which G R Townend, of 23 Ventnor Street, Leeds, placed in service in the late 1920s. It had the legend "Parlour Coach" on the side, a designation often applied to the best vehicle in the fleet by the smaller operators of that era. It had a canvas sunshine roof, shown open in this picture taken on Scarborough's Marine Drive when the vehicle was still very new. *(GHFA)*

Below: Another LTB1, built to a later specification, new in April 1931, was **EA 4833** in the Throstle Tours fleet of Walsgrove, West Bromwich. *(STA/BCVM)*

To seaside or moorland ...

Above: The driver, leaning against a lamp standard, looks exceedingly fed up as his party disembarks to sample the delights of Scarborough on a dull day in late 1929. The vehicle was **HL 4347**, No. **95** in the fleet of Bullock, of Wakefield. A May 1929 Tiger TS2, it was appropriated by the Ministry of War Transport in September 1939. *(STA/BCVM)*

Below: About as far removed from the brash Scarborough ambience as it would be possible to imagine, this picture illustrates Alexander's LTB1 Lioness No. **194** (**MS 9111**) on touring work in the autumn of 1930. The 28-seat body was by Burlingham. *(STA/BCVM)*

Signwriting par excellence ...

Above: The traditional art of the signwriter tells a story on the rear panels of Bolton independent Arthur Christy's No. **7 (WH 2477)**, a Duple-bodied Tiger TS1 28-seater, which was new in April 1930, a week or so before this photograph was taken on 6th May. The Bolton operator disposed of this fine machine in 1934. It survived with Tennant, of Forth, until December 1949. *(STA/BCVM)*

Below: A less-well known coachbuilder, Spicer, bodied this 1931 TS1 of the Southport and Birkdale Motor & Carriage Company Limited, which traded as Gore's Pullman Safety Coaches. The signwriting on **WM 6130** was equally expert. *(STA/BCVM)*

Blackpool

No choice but to
be in the open air
in Blackpool
Corporation's 34-
seat Burlingham-bodied Lion LT7
"gondola". The sun was shining, however,
and doubtless the ride was a pleasant one.
Number **115** (**FV 6125**) was new in July
1935 and lasted until 1955. One survives as
a possible restoration project. *(STA/BCVM)*

Across the other side ...

Above: Over on the east coast, at Scarborough, United Automobile Services Limited had some similar seaside buses. In 1935 ten Plaxton 35-seat bodies were ordered and fitted to 1928 ADC 425 chassis - a far cry from Blackpool's brand new Leylands (though Blackpool did have some "gondolas" on rehabilitated Lion PLSC1 chassis). The Plaxton bodies differed from Blackpool's Burlingham productions in not having open tops, although they did have two-section sliding sunshine roofs. The 1935 bodies were later mated to 1938 Tiger TS8 chassis, a combination represented by **LLS1** (**DHN 451**) at Scarborough's Corner Café terminus on a wet and windy day when the sunshine roof was doubtless firmly closed. *(R F Mack Collection)*

Below: Still in Scarborough, and back to Marine Drive, for a visitor to the resort in the shape of **DK 9849**, a 1935 Harrington-bodied 32-seater in the fleet of Charles Holt & Sons, of Whitworth. The picture was taken in July 1937. *(GHFA)*

77

Thirties development

Not much more than five years separate the dates into service of Southern National's 1930 Tiger TS2 No. **2983** (**GF 7299**) *(above)* and the magnificent Burlingham-bodied TS7 "radio coach" **DRE 605** of Hickson Bros, of Tamworth *(below)*. The Southern National vehicle, a Duple-bodied 26-seater with sliding canvas roof and two hinged doors, was outside the Southern National office in Torquay where day, half-day and evening tours were being advertised. GF 7299 was waiting to leave on such a tour to Clovelly. The Hickson vehicle was on private hire work in Nottingham circa March 1936. *(Both: GHFA)*

Variations on a Cub theme

Above: Clynog & Trevor, of Carnarvon, bought this KPZ2 Cub in August 1936. The coachwork, by R.E.A.L., of Ealing, London W5, featured a two-piece folding door for its front entrance. Curtains, high-backed seats and streamlined paintwork combine to project the appropriate image. *(STA)*

Below: The Oldham-registered **BU 7214**, a 1933 KP3 of Shaw & Sons Luxury Tours, on the other hand, had a rear entrance equipped with an inside-hung sliding door. *(STA/BCVM)*

Lions, Tigers, Lionesses and horses

Above: Not to mention LNER rolling stock... All gathered together having conveyed racegoers to the 1931 Grand National meeting at Aintree in March of that year. **CW 8266**, on the left of the picture, partially hidden by a couple of idlers and a bowler-hatted gentleman striding purposefully towards the bookmakers, was a 1928 Lion PLSC with Strachan & Brown 32-seat bodywork in the fleet of Wright, of Burnley *(see also page 58)*. The LTB1 Lioness alongside, **FV 218**, a 1929 26-seater, was owned by Hill, of Bispham. *(STA/BCVM)*

Below: A Tiger TS2 in the fleet of Bridge, of St Helens, **DJ 4447**, was having good use made of its sunshine roof. Clearly a good time was being had by all. *(STA/BCVM)*

More Lion variations

Above: This quite stunning vehicle was brand new to the J Bland, of Market Place, Grantham, fleet when photographed in April 1935 behind Grantham railway station. Given the name "Lincolnshire Princess", it was a Lion LT5A with 32-seat coachwork by Bracebridge. The nearside of the fully fronted cab was used as a baggage compartment as indicated on the door. *(GHFA)*

Below: One of the less common members of the Leyland menagerie was the Lion Cub. It was a long-wheelbase version of the standard Cub which pushed the idea of a lightweight vehicle up into the 32-seat class and led to the development of the Cheetah. Few were built. **JF 6026** was a Burlingham-bodied example in the Provincial, of Leicester, fleet. It was photographed at Huntingdon Street, Nottingham, in April 1934. *(GHFA)*

Early airline coaches

Above: The idea of coaches running in an airline's livery, so common in the postwar period, produced some attractive vehicles in the 1930s. **BGW 882** was a 1934 TS6 Tiger in the fleet of United Service Transport, of London SW17, which ran in Royal Dutch Airlines (KLM) livery. It had Harrington coachwork with only 18 seats to allow space for luggage. It was photographed at Croydon airport in 1934. *(STA/BCVM)*

Below: Harrington coachwork, this time for 25 passengers plus luggage, also graced **CLY 17**, a 1936 Tiger TS7 in the Tilling's Transport fleet. It carried Imperial Airways livery and was photographed in the forecourt of Victoria railway station in that year. This was a rare body design, with sides clearly influenced by Duple's 1935 design, though the front end retains several Harrington characteristics. *(GHFA)*

Going on holiday

Above: Suitcases waiting to be loaded stand alongside **ANN 830,** a 1934 Willowbrook-bodied Lion LT5B which was No. **7** in the fleet of Wass Bros, of Mansfield. It was one of three Wass vehicles working on hire to Trent at Huntingdon Street, Nottingham, when still very new and shiny. *(GHFA)*

Below: Queues of people, some looking rather anxious, bus company officials looking harrassed, and a Yorkshire Woollen driver, hands in pockets, bored with it all and just awaiting the signal to leave for the East Coast resorts characterise Dewsbury's 1935 wakes week, when all the factories closed down and the populace decamped to Scarborough and Bridlington, Blackpool and Morecambe. **HD 5613** was No. **333** in the YWD fleet. *(STA/BCVM)*

"Fit as a Tiger"

This remarkable vehicle, **AYM 253**, was a Tiger TS6 new in June 1934 to the Daily Mirror newspaper, of London EC4. It was bodied by Lancefield Coachworks Limited and used as a mobile fitness and gymnastics exhibition. The "Daily Mirror 8" were presumably the eight young lady instructors. In the picture above it was at Skegness in July 1934. *(GHFA; STA/BCVM)*

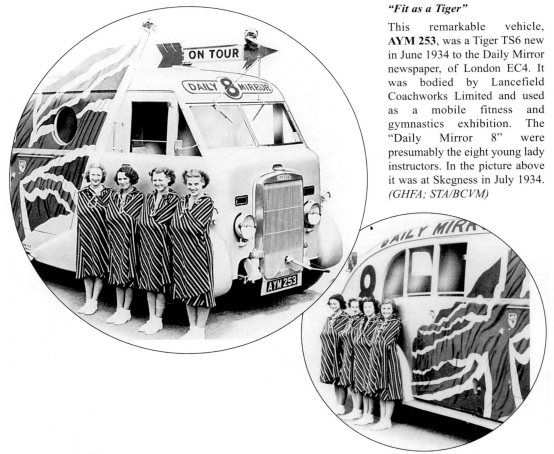

Fairground buses

The practice by travelling showmen of buying time-served buses to haul their fairground equipment around the country seems to have died out. There used to be hundreds of them, single- and double-deck, the latter often with the upper-deck windows removed and the roof lowered. They could be seen in cities, towns and villages all over Great Britain and many a driver has cursed at being caught behind an elderly Leyland Titan pulling two or three trailers. There was no "luxury" about such vehicles, but they certainly served a vast and well-patronised "leisure" activity. **NV 1039** *(above)*, a Titan TD2, had been United Counties No. 243, it was photographed at Nottingham in October 1963; Park Royal-bodied Tiger TS7 **JG 5427** was in the East Kent fleet from 1935 to 1955 *(see page 49)*. It was at Nottingham Goose Fair attempting to pull a living van out of the mud. *(Both: GHFA)*

The Original Titan

TD 9522 was the registration number carried by the first Titan. When first built *(right)* it had a Tiger-like radiator with a more rounded profile than that subsequently adopted *(above)*. The main pictures record the occasion of Leyland borrowing a 1927 Short Bros-bodied 57-seat six-wheeled Karrier DD6 double-decker, No. **53** (**FR 8379**), from Blackpool Corporation for a series of photographs to demonstrate the lower height (and, indeed, the smaller size all round for not far off the same number of passengers) of the new design. *(STA/BCVM)*

<<< *Previous page:* The first, 1927, Tiger demonstrator, **TE 1635**, illustrating the original style of radiator and badge. *(STA/BCVM)*

Titan and Titanic

Above: A whole series of demonstrators was built (the TD1 Titan alone accounted for no fewer than 14 between 1927 and 1931) for lending to potential buyers. Vehicles to improved specification were gradually made available, such as this TD1 with later style of radiator and enclosed platform and staircase, photographed on 17th September 1929. This is believed to be the bus that was sold in 1934 to Jersey Motor Transport, with whom it survived into 1960 to be the last petrol-engined double-decker in regular service in the British Isles.

Below: Three axles allowed longer vehicles and therefore more seats. The Titanic aimed to tap this market, particularly with city operators looking to replace trams. This dual-doorway vehicle, one of the series of prototypes, was built in 1927 and later sold to Sheffield. The Titanic was a poor seller and few were built. Rackham was not in favour of six-wheelers, though ironically he went on to design the AEC Renown, which was to prove the most successful British three-axle bus chassis. *(Both: STA/BCVM)*

Demonstrators in Nottingham

Nottingham Corporation was a regular user of demonstrators. A TD1 Titan 51-seater, registered **TE 2943**, which had been built in 1928, is seen *(above)* in Bentinck Road, Nottingham, on a misty, murky day in February 1929. Five years later, in better weather, a 1933 Gearless TD3c, **TJ 3278**, was in Upper Parliament Street, Nottingham *(below)*, in June of that year. This was the first TD3 and had the second prototype Leyland metal-framed body, in the same style as the production version built in 1934-6. Leyland was making much of the "Gearless Bus" idea on the side panels. More accurately described as torque-converter transmission, it was a good system, and made life easier for the driver, but at the cost of higher fuel consumption, lack of engine braking and a certain "fussiness" about climbing gradients. Most gearless buses were later fitted with conventional gearboxes. Nottingham went on to buy AEC Regents. *(GHFA Collection/Nottingham Journal; GHFA)*

Life after demonstration

Demonstrators could be expected to be maintained by the factory in first-class condition and they were a good buy for the operator seeking a bargain. County Motors Limited, of Choppington, Northumberland, was a great collector of ex-demonstrator double-deckers: AEC and Daimler as well as Leyland. The vehicle above, **TF 5988**, was built in 1931 with a dual-doorway body. Quickly converted to front-entrance specification, as seen above, it was sold to County in 1933. It passed to United Automobile Services Limited in 1934 and was again rebuilt, as a conventional rear-entance bus. **TF 9947** *(below)* was a TD2 built in 1932. It had the first Leyland metal-framed body and was to highbridge (or "Hybridge", in an early example of deliberate mis-spelling for publicity purposes) layout. It also went to County in 1933 and to United the following year. It ran in this form until rebodied by Eastern Coach Works in 1949, then becoming lowbridge. *(Both: STA/BCVM)*

Gearless single-deckers

The torque-converter transmission system was pushed hard by Leyland in the mid 1930s. London Transport was even persuaded to have ten of its 100 STD-class Titan double-deckers so fitted. In an age when clutches and manual gearshifts on buses are more often found in transport museums than in public service, it is hard to imagine the uphill struggle of earlier decades faced by manufacturers promoting more driver-friendly systems. Like the TD3c on page 89, this Tiger TS6c left the public in no doubt that something new and special was being offered. **TJ 3279** was built in 1933 and is seen in that year *(above)* at Huntingdon Street, Nottingham. It was on trade plates and it is not certain to whom it was being demonstrated. In the picture below, the bus is seen in 1934, before being sold to Clydebank Motors. It later passed to Central SMT and the Leyland 32-seat body, the third metal-framed prototype, was replaced by a double-deck Alexander unit in 1945. *(GHFA; STA/BCVM)*

Cubs and Cheetahs

Above: The range of smaller models also had their demonstrators; at least six Cubs are recorded. Not much is known for certain about this dual-door example. The slam doors and padded seats suggest coach rather than bus use, and the picture was taken on 25th July 1931. *(STA/BCVM)*

Below: The Leyland Cheetah was a lightweight but full-sized model. The eight-stud Cub wheels gave the game away, although otherwise the vehicle resembled the Lion LT7. This one, which was bodied by Leyland, was an LZ2 built for the 1935 Commercial Motor Show, at which the model was launched. *(STA/BCVM)*

TROLLEYBUSES

Leyland built up a substantial portfolio of loyal customers at home and overseas for its trolleybuses as that estimable form of traction expanded in the 1930s, often in replacement of trams. Leyland's slogan "Bury a Tram with a Titan" could well have had the word "Trolleybus" substituted for "Titan". The Portsmouth example below, No. **5** (**RF4653**), was a TBD2 model of 1934, fitted with English Electric 52-seat bodywork. *(STA/BCVM)*

Trolleybuses in Birmingham

Above: The fact that one of these vehicles sweeping up to a bus stop would betray no internal combustion engine noise would tell most people that here was something new. But six-cylinder petrol engines were smooth and silent and perhaps it was easy to be deceived. There was in fact no reason at all why a trolleybus should not have had a radiator grille air intake - electrical equipment also needed cooling. **OV 4001**, No. **1** in the Birmingham Corporation fleet, was a 1932 Short Bros-bodied TBD1. A 48-seater, it ran until 1940. *(GHFA)*

Below: **OV 1175** was a TBD1 demonstrator which was lent to Birmingham from May to August 1931. It had Leyland 48-seat bodywork and was thus even closer in appearance to the petrol-engined Titan. In this view, taken on 8th April 1932, it was being demonstrated to Chesterfield Corporation. *(STA/BCVM)*

Trolleybus design development

Above: **TJ 939** was built in 1932 and took to the roads not long after the bonneted examples with their dummy radiators shown in the previous page. A TTB model, with Leyland's own bodywork, it is seen in Parliament Street, Nottingham, in May 1933, being demonstrated to that enterprising municipality. It was in Birmingham Corporation livery. *(GHFA)*

Below: The same vehicle, a few days later, on 1st June 1933, on demonstration in Birmingham, who later bought a batch of 50 TTBs. In this view a large notice in the back window urges caution because the driver is under instruction. *(STA/BCVM)*

Nottingham and Bradford

Above: Nottingham Corporation bought a batch of 30 TTB4 trolleybuses in 1935. They were fitted with Metropolitan-Cammell Carriage and Wagon Company bodywork seating 68. Number **135 (ATV 198)** was in the city centre on 25th October 1935. It was withdrawn in 1951. *(GHFA)*

Below: Some early single-deck Leyland trolleybuses for Bradford Corporation were based on PLSC1 Lion chassis supplied without engines and gearboxes to English Electric in Preston, who then fitted 60hp electric motors and built the bodywork. Bradford's No. **544 (KW 2601)**, one of the batch of 16, entered service in February 1928 and was withdrawn in 1940. *(STA/BCVM)*

St Helens and Hull

Above: Number **125** (**DJ 6123**) of St Helens Corporation was a TBD2, new in July 1934, with 50-seat body by Brush, of Loughborough. Unusually among trolleybus systems, St Helens had a bridge clearance problem and thus required lowbridge layout. Number 125 was rebodied to similar specification by East Lancashire Coachbuilders in August 1945 and lasted in service until February 1952, when it was withdrawn and scrapped. The vehicle behind, No. **117** (**DJ 6052**), was a Ransomes D4, also Brush-bodied. *(STA/BCVM)*

Below: Kingston upon Hull Corporation's No. **2** (**CRH 926**), a TB2, was new in June 1937 with Weymann 54-seat bodywork. It was withdrawn in 1953. *(STA)*

"Ahead of its time ..."

Despite **TJ 9010**'s many admirable features and the obvious efficiency with which it could handle heavy loadings in city use in what was claimed to be greater safety, it remained unique, or as the French would say: "it had no tomorrow". Leyland produced this low-floor Type TTL trolleybus with rear entrance and front exit in 1936. Unusually for a Leyland prototype, body construction was commissioned from Massey Bros. The low floor layout required two motors, each driving the wheels on one side of the rear bogie, which would have made it more costly to build and maintain. It is seen in Walkden on demonstration/test on the South Lancs system, another user of lowbridge trolleybuses and joint operator with St Helens on the route from Atherton. *(STA/BCVM)*

London Transport trolleybuses

There is no doubt that the London trolleybus fleet at its height was a wonder to behold. The largest in the country, it was also for some the most glamorous. Not far off half of London's total of 1,891 trolleybuses were of Leyland manufacture and they were in the majority among those purchased by the LPTB from 1935 to 1942. Numbers **73/93 (CGF 73/93)** *(above)* were short-wheelbase 60-seaters with Birmingham Railway Carriage & Wagon Company bodies and Metrovick electrical equipment. They are seen at Crystal Palace on the Sutton to West Croydon route 654 in February 1936. In the same month *(below)* Nos **100/3 (CGF 100/3)** were tailgating on the isolated Bexleyheath system, respectively on the 696 to Dartford and the 698 to Bexleyheath. These vehicles were Brush-bodied. *(STA/BCVM)*

London Transport trolleybuses

Above: Most of London's trolleybuses were standard 70-seaters. This one, No. **384** (**CUL 384**), was unique in that it was the only member of London's D1 class. Built to LPTB specification, it also set the standard for Leyland's new metal-framed double-deck bus body as introduced in 1936. It was a Leyland-bodied machine with Metrovick electrical gear. It worked from Bexleyheath depot in 1936/7 and is seen here passing through Crayford on the 696, heading from Dartford towards the Woolwich Ferry. *(STA/BCVM)*

Below: A scene not too often recorded. The manufacturer's lorry, a Leyland Beaver, tows a brand new London Transport trolleybus, No. **665** (**DLY 665**), on its delivery journey on 18th June 1937. Number 665 was in London's F1 class, and had Leyland 70-seat bodywork. *(STA/BCVM)*

London Transport trolleybuses

Above: This one was irresistible. Dobbin heads towards the cameraman at a dignified trot, one eye looking straight into the lens; the smartly turned-out driver of the LMS dray attempts to look suitably aloof; a magnificent Daimler limousine hides in the background; London's Holborn architecture provides a suitable backcloth. Oh, yes, there are a couple of trolleybuses, too. Numbers **1088** and **1102** were K1-class all-Leyland vehicles heading out of the city respectively to Waltham Cross and Wood Green. The run out into the country at Waltham Cross was a long haul and one of the system's most entertaining trolleybus rides. *(STA/BCVM)*

Below: Another K1, No. **1285** (**EXV 285**), in brand new condition on 1st February 1939. The K-class all-Leyland trolleybuses had an excellent reputation, some running to almost the end of trolleybus operation in the Capital in 1962. *(STA/BCVM)*

Trolleybus demonstrators

Above: Single-deck trolleybuses were much less common than the double-deck variety; nevertheless Leyland thought it worth having a single-deck demonstrator. It was photographed on 8th September 1933 running on test under the wires of the South Lancashire Transport system at Worsley. *(STA/BCVM)*

Below: In 1938 Leyland built a 30ft-long twin-steering trolleybus with bodywork outwardly resembling that being supplied in hundreds to London Transport although it was of integral construction. It was demonstrated to that operator before being purchased. **DTD 649** became LPTB No. **1671** and was classified X7. *(STA/BCVM)*

Leylands

IN LONDON

London was a hive of Leyland activity in the period from 1925 to 1940. In the mid 1920s the independent operators placed great faith in the LB5 type to combat the London General's ponderous NS types and they were equally appreciative of the Titan's abilities pitted against the later STs and LTs of their powerful competitor. The London Passenger Transport Board, formed in 1933, eventually acquired 295 Leylands from the independents and during the remainder of the decade some standard LPTB classes were based on Lancastrian chassis. **GC 3172**, seen sweeping majestically past Marble Arch on 12th March 1931 on route 73 to Stoke Newington, was one of nine Titan TD1s in the Westminster fleet. It was bodied by Christopher Dodson, of Willesden, in north-west London, and had been new in January 1930. Upon absorption into the London Transport fleet in July 1934 it was given the bonnet number TD94 and is noteworthy in being one of four TD-class buses fitted with Leyland oil engines in October 1934 - nine of the class were running with oil engines in their later years with London Transport. *(STA/BCVM)*

Ahead of the General ...

No doubt these pictures were carefully composed to ensure that Leyland buses were "in the lead", but in truth the Titans ran rings round the General's solid-tyred early 1920s vehicles and in so doing - because they were comfortable, too - attracted no little loyal patronage from satisfied customers. Sufficient, in fact, to worry the General's management into producing a series of sumptuously appointed new buses on AEC Regent and Renown chassis: chassis designed, ironically, by G J Rackham, the Titan's creator, after he had moved south to take up an appointment with AEC. Arthur Partridge, under the fleetname "Express", had been the first to challenge the General's monopoly after the First World War; he did nothing by halves, and dared to run his buses on the prestigious route 11. His 1929 Dodson-bodied TD1, **UW 6987**, is seen *(above)* being closely followed by a General NS (both going to Liverpool Street) in the Strand in January 1930. Later that month another Westminster TD1, **UW 2308**, was heading *(below)* for Hammersmith on the 73. These buses became London Transport's TD88/101. *(STA/BCVM)*

Right: The City Motor Omnibus Co. Ltd had a fine fleet of Leylands, including three magnificent, but oddly dated-looking, Dodson-bodied Titanics (Chiswick had arrived at the sloping front STL by about the same date). **TS1 (AGH 149)** was at Victoria *(right)* when brand new in 1933. The three Titanics were oil-engined when new, but in 1935/6, by then in LPTB ownership, were converted to petrol; the oil engines went into TD-class Titans. *(Omnibus Society)*

Below: This six-wheeler was of City's own construction based on an earlier Leyland chassis. **CS4 (GP 127)** had a Ransomes body seating, like the Titanic, 62. *John Banks Collection)*

Ex-Independent Titans in the London Transport fleet

Above: The City Motor Omnibus Company Limited also had numerous Titans. London Transport **TD114** (**GO 1346**) had been City's fleet number T5. Described as a "TD Special", it had a Dodson 56-seat open-staircase body and by the time of this photograph had received a radiator from an earlier Titan.

Below: A later, enclosed staircase body from Christopher Dodson graced **TD130** (**MV 1376**), a 1932 Titan TD2, which came to the LPTB from the Prince Omnibus Company Limited. Prince was the last central area London Independent to pass to the new London Transport, on 5th December 1934. TD130 was at Wembley Stadium in about 1937. *(Both: John Banks Collection)*

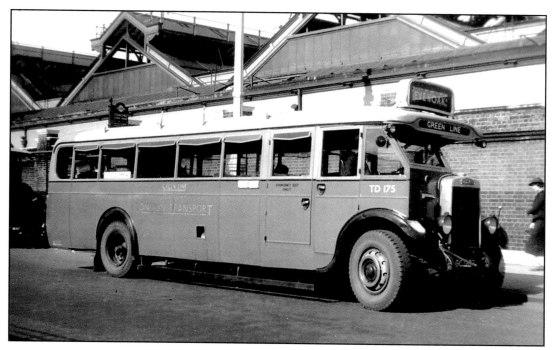

Ex-Independent single-deckers

Above: **TD175 (GC 1207)** was one of tbe few Titans to be built as single-deckers. It was one of a number which had been operated as express coaches by Premier Line Limited. It had a Duple 26-seat coach body and was put to work by the LPTB in the Green Line fleet. *(John Banks Collection)*

Below: **TR9c (UR9621)**, a 1931 Leyland Tiger TS1 with Thurgood 32-seat coachwork, had been new in 1931 to C Aston, of Watford. The vehicle passed to London General Country Services on 9th May 1933 and thence to the LPTB on its formation on 1st July 1933. TR9 was withdrawn in 1938. It is seen in the later standard prewar coach livery with both GREEN LINE and LONDON TRANSPORT transfers. *(J F Higham)*

108

<< **Opposite page: UR 6730** had passed to London General Country Services Limited in May 1933, just before the formation of the LPTB. It was a 1930 TD1 also originally owned by Aston and had a body built by Dodson to a design quite different from those running in central London. It is seen in green and black livery without a fleet number. London Transport would later number it TD171. *(J F Higham)*

Above: VX 4069 was an LTB Lioness which came to the LPTB from Harris's Coaches, of Grays, in May 1934. Though repainted in Country Area livery and operated for a short time, it was never given a fleet number and was withdrawn in 1936. *(D W K Jones)*

Below: LN1 (MT 2992) was a 1929 Dodson-bodied 32-seat PLSC3 Lion. It was acquired from G H Allitt and Sons Limited in December 1933 and ran until 1936. *(D W K Jones)*

London Cubs

Above: Although very much wedded to AEC for most of its bus and coach chassis requirements, London Transport did not hesitate to go elsewhere when the AEC range could not provide exactly what was wanted. Thus when small buses were needed, mainly to replace the mixed collection of such buses on a variety of non-standard chassis, the Leyland Cub was chosen, although in LGOC days Chiswick had favoured Dennis for earlier small buses. The first Cub, **C1 (AYV 717)**, was bodied at Chiswick and tried out in Central Area service before the decision to order Cubs in quantity was taken. *(John Banks Collection)*

Below: Eight SKPZ2 Cubs with Park Royal half-deck bodies were bought in 1936 for use on the inter-station service. **C113 (CLX 550)** is pictured at Chiswick Works. *(John C Gillham)*

TFs and CRs

Above: London Transport's TF class of underfloor-engined Tigers, jointly developed by Leyland and the Board's engineers, were startlingly modern and, but for the war, would have been the precursors of an earlier switch to this configuration than was the case. They were fitted with Chiswick-built bodies and allocated to Green Line coaching duties. **TF69c (FJJ 766)** is seen after conversion to a wartime ambulance. *(John Banks Collection)*

Below: The CR class was equally revolutionary, but it is probably fair to say that it was less successful than the TFs. Again, had the war not intervened... These rear-engined Cubs are epitomised by **CR43 (FXT 149)** photographed at Chiswick Works. *(John C Gillham)*

This page: In 1937 London Transport placed 100 Titan TD4s in service. The first 90 had crash (or "clash" as Chiswick officially referred to them) gearboxes; the remaining ten were TD4c models with torque-converter transmission: "Gearless" buses, although Leyland did not succeed in having the "Gearless" badge on the London radiators and, indeed, standard gearboxes were fitted in 1939. **STD26 (DLU336)**, when brand new, was working service 16 *(above)*. The Leyland bodywork, although in most respects a standard product, was cosmetically modified to make it resemble a contemporary STL. Indeed, a doctored photograph exists *(see below)*, presumably created for publicity purposes, of an STL with a Titan radiator grafted on, and it is difficult to detect the deception *(GHFA; STA/BCVM)*

>> *Opposite page:* About 40 years ago the writer was given this picture of Oxford Street in 1937 as a vast framed enlargement. It still hangs on the study wall and is among his favourite bus pictures. Amid all the AECs, two of the 1937 STDs, **STD42/65 (DLU 352/75)**, lead the way, followed by an ex-Independent TD. The STD-class Leylands, so much in the minority in the London Passenger Transport Board's vast fleet, made a considerable impact on the scene, running as they did through the West End to London Bridge and to Victoria. *(John Banks Collection)*

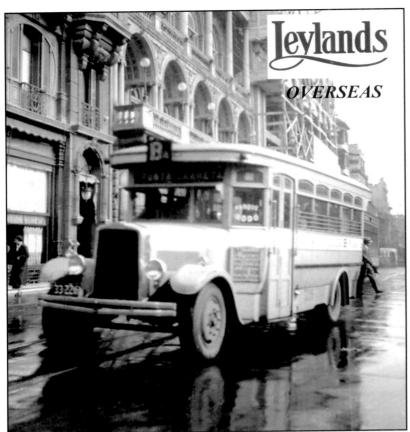

Leylands
OVERSEAS

The Leyland *marque* was as much a part of the tranport scene in dozens of overseas countries as it was in Great Britain and in this section we illustrate a fascinating selection, starting with two pictures, taken during a stroll through the streets of the Argentinian city of Montevideo on a damp day in 1936, of Leylands in service.

Left: A Cub with the registration number **33 226** was displaying a route letter B and was bound for the Porta Carreta. *(STA)*

Below: The Lioness registered **33 029**, with the prominent fleet number **9** on the radiator, was on service L to Plaza Zabala. The buses were apparently from different operators' fleets. *(STA)*

Leylands in the desert

Above: Rifle-toting policemen mounted on camels regard the cameraman with some suspicion as he takes a picture of a Leyland Cub on duty in the northern-central part of Egypt. The vehicle was operating a service between Fayoum and Bemsouef via Giza. *(STA/Abou Seada Fayoum)*

Below: A Bloemfontein, South Africa, Municipality 38-seat LTB1 Lioness seems to have been abandoned. The gentlemen on horseback with scarves covering the lower half of their faces look like highwaymen, but perhaps they were simply protecting themselves from the dust. *(STA)*

Cubs and Lionesses in Spain

Above: The Cub abroad often took on duties that would have been given to a larger vehicle in Britain. This LKP3 of 1932, **M-43078**, had heavy looking bodywork (although the low roof line and shallow windows gave an illusion of size) was clearly expected to carry a lot of luggage as well as passengers, as evidenced by the roofrack and steps leading up to it. It was photographed in Madrid to a background of typical pre-civil-war architecture. *(STA/Otto Wunderlich)*

Below: Much the same thing, writ larger, in the form of a 1931 LTB1 Lioness for service in Spain. Whereas the Cub above was left-hand-drive, this Lioness was to the British right-hand layout. Curtains and padded seats suggest use on long distance services. *(STA/BCVM)*

Lionesses on the American continent

Above: Fleet number **50** of Auto Omnibus "La Internacional", Buenos Aires, a 30-seater with locally built bodywork, was the first oil-engined Leyland in the Argentinian capital. A cast plate on the bonnet-side proudly proclaims "El Omnibus Ingles Leyland". The proprietor looks suitably proud of his new acquisition. *(STA/H G Olds)*

Below: At the northern end of the continent, in Canada, the Three Rivers Traction Company's fleet number **110** was a Lioness with C C & F Metal Works 29-seat dual doorway bodywork. The vehicle was completed and entered service in June 1934. *(STA)*

Durban trolleybuses

Above: In 1934 the Durban municipality took delivery of a batch of Leyland-GEC trolleybuses with Park Royal bodywork. Numbers **16/7** are seen on the dockside after unloading from the ship which had conveyed them from England. *(STA/BCVM)*

Below: Another of the batch is about to be towed off the dock by an elderly (even then), solid tyred Leyland lorry. *(STA/BCVM)*

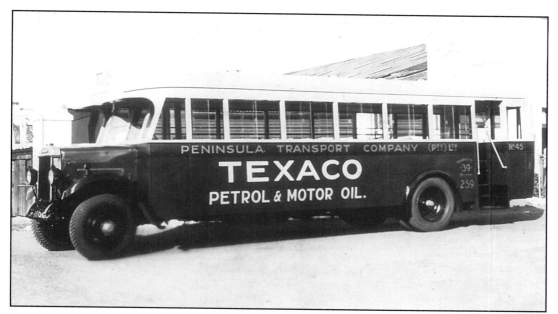

South African contrasts

Above: This remarkable vehicle, photographed in Cape Town in October 1933, was a Leyland Badger which was altered to a 39-seater by fitting a Lion frame. It was owned by the Peninsula Transport Company (Pty) Ltd. The extremely bright sunlight to some extent disguises that this was a bonneted vehicle. *(STA)*

Below: Bloemfontein Municipality added this "Gearless" Tiger TS8c to its fleet as No. **7** in 1937. It was photographed before being shipped out to South Africa. The bodywork was by Leyland. The deeper radiator with sloping face was used in some export markets, giving a look reminiscent of contemporary Daimler buses. *(STA/BCVM)*

The Rawalpindi Omnibus Service ran this 25-seat KP3 Cub on the Peshawar to Murree service. A legend on the side panels states that the speed limit for the bus was 25mph on the plains and 15mph in the hills. The photograph was taken near Bara Fort in August 1932. *(STA/BCVM)*

India and Egypt

Above: The Oankar fleet, headquartered in Calcutta, included **98-Y**. A vehicle of ungainly, top-heavy appearance, it was based on a PLSC3 Lion chassis. The locally built bodywork probably had seats for about 50, though the vehicle doubtless carried twice that number at need. The photograph was taken in 1929. *(STA/BCVM)*

Below: This dual-door, left-hand-drive Cub was intended for operation in Alexandria. It was photographed in 1932 before being shipped out to Egypt. *(STA/BCVM)*

Cubs alongside - and on - the railway tracks

Above: With a party of dignitaries and soldiers looking on, this left-hand-drive LKP3 Cub was photographed somewhere in Greece in July 1934. *(STA)*

Below: Perhaps the most unusual Leyland to feature in this book. Buses adapted to run on rails were not new in 1934, but they were never common. The New Zealand State Railways acquired this 8-seat Cub in that year. It is said to have been capable of a "remarkable performance". *(STA)*

A 1935 view of two vehicles in the L J Keys, of Wellington, New Zealand, fleet. The Leyland Cub looks to be in pristine condition. Its neighbour, of unknown chassis make, was less so, and was perhaps being replaced by the Cub. (ST4)

On this and the opposite page are two SKP3 Cubs in the fleets of New Zealand operators. Number **12 (P.526)** in the Midland Motorways fleet and No. **2** in that of the Peninsula Motor Service Limited were bodied locally to - for the era - futuristic designs which bore more than a passing resemblance to contemporary Holland Coachcraft products in the United Kingdom. These vehicles were 25-seaters and the pictures were taken in 1935. *(STA)*

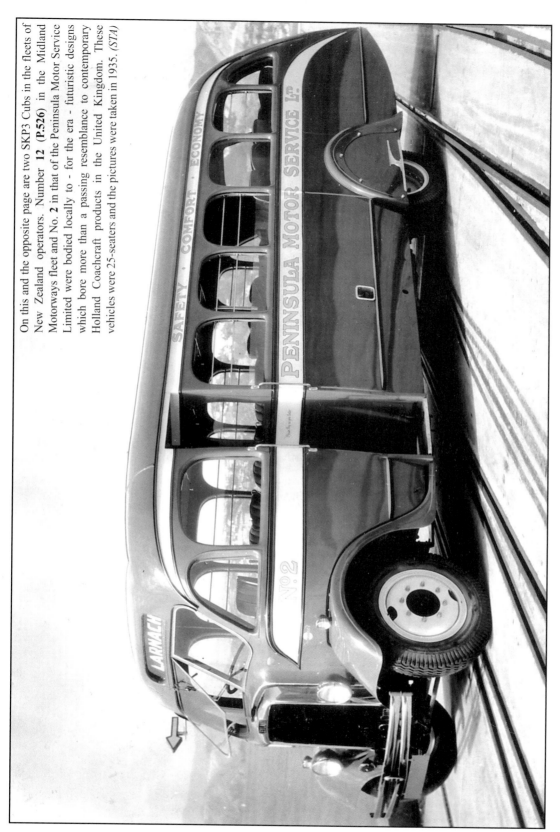

Leylands in Australia

Above: An immaculately presented and positioned fleet of ten KP3 Cubs, registered **220-931** to **940**, of the Melbourne & Metropolitan Tramways Board, photographed in 1935. The additional cast Leyland nameplate attached to the bonnet-side is noteworthy. Part of the duties for these small buses was to act as feeders to the operator's busy tram services. *(STA/E G Adamson)*

Below: One of a large fleet of Tiger oil-engined single-deckers in service in Sydney in 1938. The vehicle was bodied locally to dual-doorway specification and was part of the fleet of the New South Wales Department of Road Transport. *(STA/W A Webber)*

Leylands in Australia

Above: A Sydney operator, A Martin, ran this 26-seat Cub with dual-door bodywork of local manufacture. The vehicle is thought to have been new in 1937. *(STA/Hall & Co)*

Below: A 1935 Titan TD3c (and therefore a "Gearless" bus with torque-converter transmission) in the fleet of the New South Wales Department of Road Transport. The 56-seat body was built by S J Wood, of Sydney, to a style - apart from the plethora of sliding windows - reminiscent of Leyland's own vee-front style of that time. *(STA)*

A magnificent line-up of oil-engined Titans in the New South Wales Department of Transport's fleet in 1937. At least the leading bus, **MO 1413**, was fitted with torque-converter transmission.

(STA/Sydney Morning Herald)